your digital life
a teen's guide to the online world

josh gunderson

Copyright © 2021 Josh Gunderson

All rights reserved. No part of this book may be reproduced in any form or by any electronic or mechanical means, including information storage and retrieval systems, without permission in writing from the author, except by a reviewer who may quote brief passages in a review.

First edition.

Author Photo: Monica Poulin

ISBN: 979-8-5274-7295-0

contents

To Ollie & Jackie

*I'm sorry if your parents being strict is my fault,
just remember that I'm the cool uncle that takes
you to Disney World.*

a welcome letter to parents, guardians and educators

Hello, parents!

If we haven't met before, it's probably best that I take a moment to introduce myself. My name is Josh Gunderson and I am the author of this book! Since 2009, I have had the pleasure of travelling around the world as an educational speaker, specializing in Internet safety and bullying prevention. Since that first workshop in April, 2009, I have presented to over one million students, educators and parents. I have presented workshops and assemblies in libraries, church basements and even someone's living room!

In 2017, I released my first book <u>Cyberbullying: Perpetrators, Bystanders, and Victims</u> to help parents and educators navigate the complicated world of bullying in the online world. I wrote that first book because I felt like I never had enough time during parent workshops to get out everything I'd like to say. Most of these sessions average around 60 minutes and that is never enough time, especially since I know parents have a ton of questions for me.

So, here we are now. I'm writing to you first because I can only really assume that you either purchased this book for your teen to look over, or you purchased for yourself for the same reasons. Perhaps you stumbled upon this book while searching online; maybe a blogger wrote about it, or maybe you picked it up at one of my workshops. Whatever the reason, we are on this journey together and I am honestly excited and honored that you chose me to lead you on the way.

You've taken the perfect first step towards working with your teen to understand the ins and outs of the online world. Believe it or not, I'm not talking about buying this book! I'm talking about the fact that it showed up in the mail, and you took the time to crack it open and start reading for yourself!

This is what you should be doing when it comes to technology and what apps your kids are using. As they want to download new apps or join new social networking sites, you should be taking the time to get to know what they are getting themselves into. Learn the rules of the app, the privacy settings and stay knowledgeable about any issues in the news when it comes to that particular app. If you have concerns, share them with your child in an honest and constructive conversation. If it's a lecture, they aren't going to listen; have it be a conversation with give and take.

Something you should know about me is that I am big on communication, especially when it comes to the parent/child relationship. More so when it comes to the wide, scary world of the Internet and social media. Reading this ahead of or along with your child is key to facilitating constructive conversations about the online world. Doing this gives you the ability to sit down and chat about something you have learned or something they picked up during their time with this book. Was there new information? Was there something that was unclear? Did Josh make too many *Jurassic Park* references?

Things like that!

Communication is key and it is my hope that both you and your child are able to use this book as a stepping stone to opening that door.

breaking down digital walls

Parenting in a world where everyone is connected to one another 24/7 is frustrating! I know this because I've seen it first hand on the faces of every parent, guardian, and educator that comes to one of my workshops. In the grand scheme of things, there are millions of apps and social media platforms out there in the cyber world, and while many fall into obscurity, a number of them seem to rise up and take over the entire world. For the longest time it seemed like Instagram was the top dog, but, as of sitting down to write this, TikTok is the king.

This is actually a big part of the reason why I've always been super hesitant to sit down and write a full-blown book on what parents should know about all these things because by the time I'm done writing, a majority of them would be obsolete!

On my end, the absolute truth of the matter is that even I am not up to date on everything going on with social media and apps. It would be virtually impossible to keep up with them all and have on-hand knowledge available to me at all times. Instead, I pay close attention to what is gaining the most attention, either positive or negative, and I focus my energy on that. Most of the time, I'm learning about new apps and sites from students that I am working with, which leads me to very important tip number one for parents:

Talk to your kids!

Ask them if they've seen any funny videos or awesome memes online lately. There's a great chance that they're going to open an app you've never heard of to show you something new. Taking an interest like this as opposed to just going through their phones will go a long way! Who knows, maybe they'll introduce you to something you'll enjoy as well!

There's also a very good chance they'll introduce you to an absolutely annoying earworm of a song that will burrow its way into your brain and keep you up all hours of the night. Yes, I'm thinking of a very specific TikTok song right now, but I will not burden you with which song it is. I'll let your kids curse you with it.

Now don't get me wrong; I love my devices as much as the next person, but I have seen how our technology is becoming a major point of contention in many relationships and households. That might have something to do with how much time we are logging onto our devices every day.

According to a census conducted by Common Sense Media in 2019, teenagers ages 13-18 are spending an average of over seven hours on their phones per day with tweens (ages 8-12) not far behind with an average of almost five hours.[1] These findings aren't even factoring in time spent on homework, reading, or taking in different forms of entertainment like videos and music. Add those in, and you see those numbers jump to almost ten hours logged for teens and nearly six for tweens.

I'm sorry to say that adults are just as guilty of the crime of spending too much time with their noses buried in devices. I'm including myself in this, I promise! The cold hard facts are we are spending, on average, over nine hours a day on our digital devices, according to another report from Common Sense Media.[2]

There's no denying or escaping the fact that technology has become a major part of our lives. There are very few opportunities to get away from it, short of climbing Mount Everest where I'm 99% sure you won't be able to get a cell signal...

Whelp, that started as a joke, but then I just searched it and it turns out you can not only get reception on Mount Everest, but you'll enjoy some good ole 5G network connections while you're up there, according to an article I found online,[3] so there really is no escaping it. I don't know why that makes me sad right now. Probably because it's further proof that everyone, but me, was being super productive during COVID-19 lockdowns.

What that means for us adults out there is we have no choice but to accept that, at some point, our young ones will have their hands on a digital device at some point in their lives. The best thing we can all do is work to provide them with the best tips, tricks and advice that we can on how to conduct themselves in the online world.

That's what I've been working hard to do for the past decade as I've worked with countless students of all ages; that's my goal for writing this book. To offer up the best advice possible, not only to the teens you bought this book for, but for you as well. Believe it or not, most kids these days are more open to new information and ideas than you could possibly imagine. It's all about the delivery!

Think about your mentality when you were their age, or even now as an adult. We all hold onto that ideal of *"you can't tell me what to do!"* And the more someone tries to tell you what you can't do, the more inclined you are to want to do it. But what if you were presented the same ideas in a way that was more constructive?

When I'm standing in front of an audience of tweens or teens, one of the first things I do is call myself out. I'm open and candid, and say what they're all thinking, "Oh man, this guy is going to stand up there for the next hour and tell me not to do things." Then they go to the happy place in their heads full of TikToks and Fortnight.

But that's not what I'm all about, and I will be honest and tell them that. I'm not so naive as to think that by standing up there and telling them not to do things, I will be an effective educator. I know for a fact that the opposite is true. I let them know that they have a choice whether or not they want to listen to me, but my hope is that they do. From there, what they do with all of that information is entirely up to them. My only request is that they listen along and hopefully we all have a good time.

I am of the firm belief that learning does not have to be boring, and that includes when I'm sitting down and writing books like this. As an educator, I follow the wisdom of Walt Disney when he said, "I would rather entertain and hope that people learned something than educate people and hope that they were entertained." After ten years of teaching with this quote in mind, I can come to you with conclusive proof that it is possible to educate and entertain.

What I'm trying to say right now is, while I hope that you and your teens take what I have to say seriously in these pages, I really hope you are open to having some fun along the way. Within these pages I have provided the best information I can about the use of technology in your digital lives with a mix of true stories, a little bit of my weird humor, and some common sense tips I have found to be useful. I encourage notetaking while you read this book. Write down possible discussion questions and talk them over with your teen. Use these questions to listen and have those constructive conversations with them rather than sitting them down for yet another lecture. You might be surprised! They could have interpreted this book a lot differently than you did!

Now, you might have some questions for me and I would be surprised if you didn't. Good chance your questions are the same ones that I've heard a hundred times over when wrapping up parent workshops. What's so funny is most of the time, the answers I offer are never what the parents are looking for and for a very good reason. You know your kids a lot better than I do. There is no "one size fits all" when it comes to parenting. Ask any parent who has multiple kids and they will back me up on that.

Many parents want to know the best age for their kid to get a device or sign up for social media and I really don't know. I mean, I could go with the very dry and clinical answer of 13-years-old. Why 13? Because that's what the law says! Really!

I'm referring to the Child Online Privacy Protection Act (COPPA) which is a law that was passed in 1998 that prevents web sites and social media from collecting certain information from users which includes, but is not limited to their first and last names.[4] So when it comes to sites like Instagram, Facebook and TikTok it is actually illegal for children under the age of 13 to be using those platforms with or without parental consent.

No, S.W.A.T. isn't going to come bursting into your house to arrest you, your kids, and your cat because someone under 13 is using these platforms (though that would be really cool and I would like to see video of that). What happens is based entirely on the platform. For example, TikTok will allow a user to join, but the account is severely restricted to what content it can see. Additionally, users aged 13-15 are automatically set to private by default.

Social media is one thing, but devices are a whole other story. At what age should I give my child a device or cell phone of their own? I have no answers; I really don't. I didn't get my first cell phone until I was 17 and driving my own car and the phone lived in the glove box for emergencies. Granted, that was back in the Nokia days and you paid for each text message sent and received.

With more schools going 1-to-1 with devices, it's hard to put an age on it. Remote learning put a whole new spin on things when we were all living, working and learning from home. Technology, much like Thanos, is inevitable. It is a necessary tool in the world we live in. With that said, it is important that every adult in your child's life takes the responsibility of teaching them how to use that tool appropriately. Remember, it takes a village.

If it helps anything at all, I rolled my eyes writing that as much as you did reading it. But it's the honest truth. Think about it like learning to drive a car. Your kid will attend classes and lessons for learning how to drive, but that's not enough. They need practice, and that's where you come in! We all work together to make sure we are putting safe, smart drivers on the road. We need to be doing the same with our devices. If they aren't mature enough to care for and use it responsibly, they aren't old enough to have it.

By now, you're pulling your hair out and screaming, "JUST TELL ME AN AGE, JOSH!" and I'm sorry to say, I just can't do it. Putting a blanket statement down like that can cause problems because every child is different. At this point in my life, I know many adults that can't handle having a cell phone and access to social media, so how can I tell you what age is appropriate? You know your child best; follow your instincts and make sure you do your research.

If you do decide to give your child a device (phone, tablet, ipod, laptop or anything else that can connect to the Internet) then make sure that you develop ground rules for appropriate use and outline the consequences for breaking those rules. Work together to create a contract for online safety and conduct for both your child and you. At the end of the book, I've given you two sample contracts that you can use outright or as a guideline for your own. What's important is that you work together, make them a part of the process so that they understand where you are coming from with making these rules and you can also see things from their perspective.

Having them be a part of the rulemaking process will help make them feel more accountable. Additionally, have them be a part of the consequence process. Work together to create acceptable punishments for not following the rules. "By letting your child weigh in, you're giving him a sense of control, which means he'll be more likely to follow the rules you've agreed upon," says psychiatrist Dr. Stuart Goldman in a wonderful article about rule setting.[5] Remember when I said "it takes a village?" I wasn't kidding! Don't be afraid to Google search or even talk to other parents about this. Chances are, you are all in the same boat!

What's important is that you stay informed when it comes to technology, social networking and apps. It's an ever-changing world and you are going to need to stay on top of it. Pay attention to what's in the news, what your kids are talking about, and what other parents are wondering about as well. When it comes to handing over any sort of device to your child, your job is just beginning. As technology advances, as they start downloading more apps and joining more web sites and playing more games, it's up to you to be on top of all of those things.

The great thing is that there are plenty of wonderful resources available to you and web sites dedicated to educating parents about the digital world and beyond. Believe it or not, I'm not putting myself on the top of that list. While I do my best to stay on top of what's going on in the online world, I am but one man and keeping up with all of these things is a full time job. That's why I love sites like Common Sense Media where they have teams of people dedicated to researching websites, apps, and other forms of media and entertainment.

Find what works best for you and yours and roll with it!

Just remember my number one rule: communication! Look for the opportunities to have meaningful conversations with your kids about what is going on in the world. Find those teachable moments in the news or even your own lives. Hopefully this book is the first step in the right direction!

a letter to the teen readers: protecting your brand

Hello!

Please do not think for a second that I am going to spend this entire book hating on social media. First off, that's not my style by any stretch of the imagination. Secondly, I'm an avid user of social media myself! No, you're not going to find me dancing on TikTok (though I did end up joining TikTok over the course of writing this book so I sure hope you enjoy videos of cats because that's all I have to offer the world) but you will find me sharing pictures of my adventures on

Instagram, sharing stories from my life on my blog, and tweeting random thoughts out for all the world to ignore. I also fully recognize that everything I just said makes me sound old. I totally own that fact; I've come to peace with it.

I'm not here to try to be your best friend, and I promise that I'm not going to spend this entire book trying to sound hip and with it. I am neither of those things. As a student once put it, "Your meme game is stale, bro." I'm not 100% sure what that means, but I got the message, I think. Considering 85% of my communication style is through memes, I feel like my meme game is, as the kids say, "on point." I could be wrong.

My goal is to provide you with the best information possible about the great big, digital world in front of you. From there, it's up to you to decide what to do with that information. I'm not going to tell you what paths to take in life, but I am going to try very hard to give you the tools you need to forge your own path. Much like your parents or guardians and teachers, I want what's best for you.

That probably sounds a bit strange coming from someone you've likely never met, but it's the truth. I love the work of educating, no matter what form it takes. Sure, my preferred form of teaching is in front of living people where I can see and hear your reactions, but we work with what we've got. The point is that I'm here to help point you in the right direction. I, like the person who handed you this book to read, do care about you. The proof is in the pudding!*

Now that doesn't mean we can't have fun along the way! I'm going to try to keep this lighthearted when I can. My goal is to educate you, not bore you into a nap. Sure, we're going to talk about some heavy and uncomfortable things, there's no getting around that. There's your first lesson! Life is full of heavy and uncomfortable moments, but sometimes that's how we learn. When we look at the mistakes of others, we can learn from them before they become our mistakes as well. I'm also not planning on sugar coating anything. That would just be doing a major disservice to you. Life gets messy when you try to hide the truth. For that

---

* The saying "the proof of the pudding is in the eating" is first recorded in English in the early 17th century, but it is likely much older. Phrases for the notion that to taste something is to test it go back to, at least, the 14th century. But back then, no one was talking about the kind of sweet, creamy "pudding" confections we now get mostly from boxed mixes or pull-top snack containers. Puddings were gutsy (literally)! They were essentially sausages—usually mixtures of minced meat, cereal, spices, and often blood, stuffed into intestines or stomachs, and boiled or steamed. In the Middle Ages, they could be very good or very bad—or possibly fatal if the meat used was contaminated. But to find out, you had to put it to the "proof."

reason I will offer a blanket trigger warning now. While I really try to keep things light, some things just can't be made fun. We're talking about the real world here and sometimes it's really not that great. Take a deep breath and I promise we'll get through it together.

My biggest ask is you keep an open mind while you are reading. It's really easy to find yourself on the defensive when someone asks you to take a look inward which is sometimes what I'll be doing in the pages that follow. It's hard to admit that we're not perfect. I'm terrible at admitting that I have flaws, and it's something that I'm working on for myself. It's so easy to think to yourself "this doesn't apply to me" or "I already know this, why are you telling me this?"

Want to know a secret? I have seen adults have the same reaction when I say something that hits a little bit too close to home. The stories I can tell of parents getting upset with me when I give them an answer they don't like when it comes to parenting. Worse, when I offer up parenting advice as someone who doesn't have kids myself. I had one parent send me a five-page email reading me the riot act when I jokingly compared raising kids to having cats. They were not happy with me. My sister, who recently had her second child, agrees with my observation so I feel pretty vindicated in my opinion.

Know this though, I am not targeting any one specific person in what I'm talking about in the pages that follow. I'm not attacking you, your friends or your parents. That said, if you do find yourself taking umbrage with something I've said, that's the time to do a self-evaluation to figure out why you are feeling that way. We've all made mistakes and sometimes that's a hard thing to admit. Believe me, I know I'm not that great at it myself, but I am learning. Just like you.

Also know that I, myself, am not perfect. I've done some pretty stupid things in my life when it comes to the online world. Because I'm human. Sometimes that means learning from my mistakes. I've had parents (not even my parents) yell at me for things I've posted online. I've had people take offense over my use of adult language on my podcast, my writing about drugs and sex in my memoir, or the time I suggested that Elf on a Shelf was actually a murderous toy come to life to end us all while we are sleeping.

Each time I get one of these bits of feedback, I stop and do some self-assessment. Much like you, I don't like being yelled at, especially by strangers. So I look at their complaints as objectively as possible. In the case of my podcast, yep, I swear. It's nothing excessive, but I can see how someone could be offended that an educator such as myself says bad words (spoiler alert: your teachers swear, your parents swear, we all do it). People forget I'm human just the same as them. Also, reports have shown that swearing is actually a sign of intelligence as opposed to being uneducated and unable to properly convey emotion.[6]

Same goes for my memoir. I knew that when I released it, parents and educators would read it and some may not like the things that I talk about within its pages. But to not talk about them would have been a disservice to myself and my reader. It would have diminished all that I was trying to accomplish by sharing those stories in the first place. So I took the chance and put it all out there for the world to see because that was my truth and my experience and my lessons learned.

It reminds me of a time I received a speaking request from a school. They asked me what topics I would cover in my assembly workshop and I provided the breakdown of the program. I was asked to remove the section about sexting because "we don't want to give the kids any ideas." I was baffled not so much by the request, but the reasoning for it. Not talking about it doesn't make it go away or prevent it from becoming a problem. Talking about it, along with the lessons learned from it, helps prevent others from making the same mistakes. I ultimately passed on the engagement because of how censored I was asked to be for both the students and the parents. It all felt like it defeated the purpose of having the programs in the first place.

I did remove the post about Elf on the Shelf from my Instagram, though. Not so much because the parent that complained called me a "disappointment" and a "hypocrite," but because it didn't fit with the aesthetic I was going for on my feed. It was a great example about how sometimes "just joking around" doesn't work in the online world, but we'll get to that in a bit. Though, for the record, I'm still convinced that Elf on a Shelf is just a real life Chucky doll. Just like the real Anabelle doll is a Raggedy Ann and not the creepy one we see in the movies.

Why do I do this? Because everything I put out into the world via the Internet is part of my personal "brand" and I want to make sure that I am being represented in the best light. When it comes to the digital world, you need to always be thinking about your own personal brand. Every TikTok, Tweet, and Instagram Post all become a representation of you: your brand.

Think of some of the brands that you and your friends are big fans of. Marvel, Netflix, and Nintendo rank among some of the big ones among teenagers today.[7] What makes them memorable? Why do they stand out over DC, Hulu, and XBox? Do they create a superior product? Do their values align with yours? Is it because Iron Man is the superior billionaire superhero?

Now think about the celebrities or influencers that you like to follow. Who's popping into your head right now? Jojo Siwa? James Charles? Zendaya? Did one of those names, perhaps, make you cringe a little? There's a good reason for that.

James Charles is an example of someone whose personal brand was tarnished because of his actions online. The popular beauty influencer had made a name for himself on his YouTube channel which, at its peak, boasted over 25 million subscribers. In early 2021, Charles was accused of sexual misconduct including grooming[†] and sexting through social media platforms with underage users. These actions have led to Charles losing brand partnerships and the ability to make money from his videos online.[8]

This is a bit of an extreme example, but an example none the less about how your actions online can alter the course of your entire life. For example, there's the story of a young man from Texas, Justin Carter, whose entire life was changed by a status update in February 2013, landing him in hot water and facing federal charges.

Following an argument with a fellow gamer online, Carter took to Facebook and posted the follow-

---

[†] Grooming /ˈgroomiNG/ *noun* | the action by a pedophile of preparing a child for a meeting, especially via an Internet chat room, with the intention of committing a sexual offense.

ing status update, *"I'm f***ed in the head alright / I think I'ma shoot up a kindergarten / and watch the blood of the innocent rain down / and eat the beating heart of one of them."*[9] A concerned woman who saw the status update alerted the authorities leading to Carter's arrest.

In April of 2013, Justin was charged with making a terrorist threat, a third-degree felony, and held on a $500,000 bail. If found guilty of the charges, it would mean that Justin would spend a minimum of ten years in jail for the comment.[10] In 2018, Carter pleaded guilty to a Class A misdemeanor and, after five long years, he was able to move on and begin a new chapter of his life.[11] But what kind of damage has that one comment done to his personal brand? What happens when a story like this pops up in an employer's job search?

The concepts of adulthood and having a career probably seem so far away that it's not worth thinking about, but you have to remember that the Internet is forever. Your status update today might affect things one week from now. One month. One year. Even ten years from now. How many times have you seen the past tweets from celebrities come back to bite them in the behind? Learn from their mistakes before they become yours.

My ultimate goal is to give you a helping hand as you begin or continue to navigate this great big digital world we live in. It's not my intention to shame or scare anyone so much as provide you with a real world look at what is going on beyond the screens. I tell these stories because I want you to think, to have them in your head as you charge forward into the craziness of life!

Let's get to it shall we?

privacy matters

Contrary to many popular beliefs and stereotypes, teens are actually very concerned with their privacy when it comes to the online world. More than that, these platforms want their users to be safe and do everything in their power to give you the ability to keep your information safe. It really comes down to our willingness to make sure that we are being safe and smart. This becomes difficult as we move around from one platform to another, each one with its own rules and settings. Worse, when you download an update, it will undo your settings.

Not too long ago I upgraded my phone. This was my first upgrade in almost a decade. Yeah, you read that right. Almost a decade. I'm of the belief that if it ain't broke, then don't fix it. Then it broke.

A lot had changed from the last time I had bought a new phone, and I had to spend the better part of the day not only downloading all my favorite apps, but adjusting and double checking all of my privacy settings. What a nightmare that was! But it was a necessary one because I always want to be as safe as possible.

Why? While I may not be a Jonas Brother or Olivia Rodrigo, I'm often in the public eye, especially when I'm speaking to hundreds of thousands of people every year. Back in 2016 I had a situation where I was being stalked by someone. I won't go too far into the details of that case, but it was a scary time. This person knew where I lived and would use my social media posts to know when I was home or not. Even after getting the police involved, he would still follow my social media posts and use them to find where I was.

This caused a huge shift in how I chose to use social media and helped me develop a lot of the rules I share with students today. I didn't let this incident stop me from living my life, but it definitely made me more cautious when posting to my public accounts. As a general rule now, I won't post about being somewhere until I'm already gone. When I'm posting photos from home, I'm careful to take a good look at it to make sure there isn't anything too personal in the frame.

This all means taking the time to slow down and think about what I'm putting out there into the world and I encourage that for you as well. We live in a very fast-paced world where we expect everything to happen at lightning speed, but that's not always the best way to live our lives. By slowing down and taking the time to think about what we're posting, it can save a lot of headaches in the future.

An example?

I am a big fan of game nights. I love getting a group of friends together to come over and enjoy a night of laughing like buffoons over a round of Cards Against Humanity. I usually try to host a gathering like this every other month or so. Because I spend so much time away from home speaking at schools, it's my way of being able to spend time with friends.

After one of these game nights, one of my friends and I were hanging out and chatting in the living room and just catching up about life. During our chat, one of my cats jumped up onto the coffee table and began performing her shenanigans in a bid to get our attention. It worked. My friend instinctively pulled out her phone to capture the moment and share it online.

As she was adjusting the photo to fit the needs of her social media I happened to look back down at the cat who was still being adorable. She was being adorable right on top of a magazine that had just come in the mail and was sitting on the coffee table waiting to be read. On the front of that magazine? My name and address. I stopped my friend from posting and asked to see the picture and, sure enough, clear as day in the frame was that same magazine along with my address. Had I not stopped her from posting, it would have been broadcast out on her public account with several thousand followers.

I can't help but wonder what would have happened had I not looked back down at the cat on the coffee table. What would have happened if she had posted that photo for the entire world to see. Sure, there's a chance no one else would have noticed, but there's a great chance that someone would have. I'm often away from home for long periods of time and my public social media will show you as much. Someone with theft on their mind could easily put all those pieces together and wait for the opportune moment to break in.

Prior to the stalking incident, I didn't have much by way of home security. I'd like to think that the cats would do something to protect their home, but I know for a fact that two out of the three would hide somewhere because they don't like strangers and the third would likely offer to help a burglar carry things out of the house so long as they left her favorite cat perch by the window.

If you think I'm just being paranoid, I can promise you I'm not. With the advent and wide-spread use of social media sites, there has been a marked increase in home robberies[12] especially in the summer months when families are more likely to be away on vacation and sharing on social media. Without realizing it, they have turned on a welcome sign in their empty homes. This is a big reason why I always encourage audiences to hold off on posting about their vacations until they've returned home.

It's also important to think twice before logging on to brag about expensive purchases as well. Everything from sharing your PS5 to a new piece of art can lead to trouble. In Houston, TX a group of tech-savvy thiefs used information collected from social media to steal hundreds of thousands of dollars of art from homes. They would monitor social media posts, waiting for the homeowners to be at work or on vacation to strike. In one instance, these thieves saw that one homeowner was hosting a big party and they attended in an effort to case the home.[13]

I'm not telling you these stories to scare you (or your parents) but as an effort to emphasize that when it comes to privacy, just looking at your settings isn't enough. It's about taking the time to slow down and take a look at the bigger picture or, in some cases, the literal picture. Think about the story of my friend and my cat. All of the privacy settings on all of my accounts meant nothing in this instance.

Keep these stories in mind next time you're hanging out at a friend's house or when they're over at yours. Did you snap a candid photo of your friends playing a video game? Be sure to check with them before you post it or share it on social media. Be mindful of what's in the background of your photos just as much as you are the actual subject of the photo. You never know what information you may be sharing with strangers without even realizing it!

Also, be sure to take care when location tagging photos on social media. I'll use another personal example here. A friend of mine created a location tag for his home, declaring it "Major's Manor" and would often use it when tagging photos from home on Instagram, really not thinking anything of it. Then I showed him what he was actually doing. He was giving anyone that saw his account a map to his home. Literally.

When you click on the location of a photo on Instagram it will not only pull up every photo taken at that location, but will show where it is on a map. Clicking on the map will open whatever app your phone uses to give you directions. From there, it will give you the instructions on how to get from your location to the one on the map.

"In just a few clicks, I have unlocked a wealth of information about you," I told my friend. "From there it's just a matter of waiting until you post about being at work or on vacation."

As he was the owner of the house, he had chronicled his home improvements and renovations on his Instagram account which gave me a good look at everything in his home. Electronics, valuables, furniture- it was all there on full display for me and anyone else looking at his very public account. He has since removed all of those tags and switched his account to private. I should also note that I changed his last name in this story because I'm not that mean.

It's also a good idea to make sure you take a good look at your phone's location settings. When I got my new phone I forgot that every photo I took was marked with the location where it was taken for a good couple weeks. While it's great that you're able to use the "find your phone" feature for when you inevitably leave it in a bathroom at the Dallas International Airport, you don't want everything you do being tracked. Check your phone settings along with your individual apps to make sure you're not leaving a roadmap straight to you for strangers and creepers to follow.

At this point you're probably wondering if it's super annoying to be friends with an online safety specialist, and I promise you that I'm actually not that bad with my friends, but when I see a teachable moment, you better believe that I'm going to jump on it! At the same time, it's just as important to take their privacy into consideration as it is mine. We all work together to keep one another safe and smart, because sometimes I even need reminders!

The first step is simply taking a look at what settings you currently have in place across your social media platforms. Take the time to take a look at every app and site that you are using to make sure you have privacy settings enabled. Seriously, I want you to do it right now while you're thinking about it. I can wait.

You back? Awesome. Hopefully you were able to find the settings and make the adjustments necessary to keep yourself safe. Another good idea would be to go back and take a look at old posts you've made. Did you use a location tag you shouldn't have? Is there too much information revealed in a picture that you didn't realize was there? Get those out of there now before they become a problem later!

As you are downloading new apps and joining new sites, make sure you are taking the time to adjust privacy settings to the level that works for you and not just allowing the default setting to take hold. This could save you from a world of headaches in the future!

Next up is limiting who can see all of this information and your posts. I am fully aware that a public account will get more attention and likes, but is all of that worth your safety? Probably not. The higher your privacy settings, the harder it is to find you online. Make your accounts private or "friends only" and make sure it's people you know gaining access to your posts online.

The truth of the matter is, you never know who is looking at what you post online. More and more college admission officers and hiring managers are looking at what their applicants are posting online. What they are finding is leading them to reject applicants from admission or employment.[14] [15] Something as simple as a single tweet, status update or joke on Instagram can end up costing you a whole lot.

Hopefully, by this point, you've checked your privacy settings and double checked that your posts aren't revealing too much information. Next step is to go back through and look at your content as if you were that college admissions officer or future employer. Would they find that video as funny? That picture? That post? Now would be a great time to delete them from your timelines and accounts. If you need an objective eye, ask a teacher or parent what they think about a post and how it might reflect upon you.

If I could, I would give you the step-by-step instructions for each and every app and device to set up your securities and privacy settings, but that would be a whole book in and of itself. Not to mention a very tedious book for me to write and for you to read. Would anyone even buy that book? Probably not worth trying to find out. So I'm going to leave it up to you to make sure that you take the time to check out all the settings available to you with each new app you download. Don't just rush through agreeing to everything to get to the fun. Take the time to be smart and take the time to think about what you're putting out there and just who might see it.

understanding the first amendment and freedom of speech

The story of Justin Carter is one that I use often when speaking to students about online safety and digital footprints. It is a prime example of how damaging a single status update can be to someone. His is just one of many similar stories I have shared over the years. His, in particular, shows how extreme the consequences can be for online behavior, but also leaves a lasting impression with students and parents alike. It's one of the stories that I will always share with both groups in separate workshops because it's the perfect story for parents to talk with their kids about. You heard this story, I did too! What did you take away from it?

Justin's story and others like it do tend to bring up the same question from audiences of all ages and walks of life. The question of the First Amendment and freedom of speech. It's one of the few amendments that we are all familiar with, but it is often one of the most misinterpreted.

Here's what it states:

"Congress shall make no law respecting an establishment of religion, or prohibiting the free exercise thereof; or abridging the freedom of speech, or of the press; or the right of the people peaceably to assemble, and to petition the Government for a redress of grievances."[16]

What many people don't understand a good chunk of the time is there are certain instances that are not covered by the First Amendment. Cases like Justin's are often the exception to the rules, and proof that you can't actually go around saying whatever you want. Depending on who you ask, there are actually ten very specific types of speech that are not protected by the First Amendment. They are: Content Regulations, Fighting Words (Incitement), Obscenity, Child Pornography, Libel and Slander, Crimes Involving Speech, Threats, Violation of Copyright Rules, Conduct Regulations, and Commercial Speech.[17]

For the sake of everyone's sanity, I'm not going to go into depth on each of these exceptions, but I do want to talk about the ones that apply to Justin's case, as well as other topics we'll be discussing later on. I encourage you to dig deeper into the others though, because, while they may not apply to your life now, they could down the line.

FIGHTING WORDS‡:

This term refers to any speech that is used to provoke someone in a way that would incite physical retaliation. This also refers to any speech that would promote imminent lawless action. Think of it as screaming "FIRE!" in a crowded movie theatre, also known as incitement. If you incite violence or encourage a mass of people to commit illegal acts, you are not covered by freedom of speech.

There was a lot of talk of this particular exception in January, 2021 after the riots at the U.S. Capitol Building following a speech by then-president, Donald

---

‡ Bonus points to anyone who's brain went to old Looney Tunes cartoons and heard Yosemite Sam's "them's fighting words!" in your head. Because it happened to me. If you don't know what I'm talking about, it's on YouTube. Take a break from the book and go search it! But make sure you come back, don't fall down a rabbit hole and end up still on YouTube in an hour crying over Golden Buzzer Videos from America's Got Talent. I'm mostly talking to myself at this point but we've all been there.

Trump. Many felt his speech on the morning of January 6, along with his tweets before and after the rally, incited the violence that took place that day. Others likened the speech and subsequent legal attacks against Donald Trump to the case of Brandenburg v. Ohio,[18] claiming there was nothing inflammatory about the speech and tweets.

I'm not here to debate politics, but this is what we refer to in the business as a "teachable moment" and, like I've said, I'm not one to let those go to waste. If you're going to reference rules that were written a couple hundred years ago, it's important that you fully understand them. Trust me when I say that I am just as guilty of throwing around the "First Amendment" argument without understanding what I was talking about. It really didn't help that the assistant principal at my high school was a studied expert on the U.S. Constitution.

Awkward.

But while we're on the topic, we might as well talk about Donald Trump's subsequent removal and banning from platforms like Twitter, Facebook, Snapchat and even TikTok. Many felt that doing so was a violation of the freedom of speech.[19] Not really the case, but we are getting into very interesting, uncharted territory. You have to remember that social media and the Internet haven't been around all that long. There's a good chance your parents grew up in a time when the Internet didn't exist and we had to turn to channel 3 to play video games. It was a dark time.

The First Amendment protects citizens from censorship by the U.S. Government, not from private companies like Twitter. Like the rest of us, Donald Trump had to agree to certain terms of service and agreements when signing up for social media platforms. There is no special agreement for celebrities or politicians; we all click the same box under the same terms. If the platform feels that a user violates those terms of service, the platform is well within their rights to suspend or ban the user. Honestly, if Twitter wanted to remove my account right now because they felt like it, they could. I'm not saying that would be very nice or fair, but it is within their rights as a private company.

Now, if the government were to go to Twitter and tell them to shut down my account because they didn't like me criticizing them, *that* would be a violation of my freedom of speech. That's the important difference in a case like this or any case of freedom of speech. It applies to government censorship. So yeah, we have the freedom to say whatever we'd like, but we need to be ready to face the consequences of those words.

THREATS:

Another quick history lesson! In August, 1966, 18-year-old Robert Watts was attending a protest and discussing police brutality. During a conversation, Watts said, "I have already received my draft classification as 1-A and I have got to report for my physical this Monday coming. I am not going. If they ever make me carry a rifle, the first man I want to get in my sights is L.B.J."[20]

Watts was arrested and convicted of violating a statute from 1917 which prohibits any person from "knowingly and willingly [making] any threat or to take the life or to inflict bodily harm upon the President of the United States."[21] While the Supreme Court did reverse the decision in the conviction of Watts in 1969, it did set the precedent for what would be known as the "True Threat Doctrine." The court established that there is a true threat exception to protected speech, but that the statement needed to be viewed in its original context and be distinguished from protected hyperbole.

In the case of Watts v. United States, the court determined that Watts' statement, when considered in context along with the laughter it received from the crowd, was more "a kind of very crude offensive method of stating a political opposition to the President" than a "true threat".[22]

Why am I telling you all of this? It's mostly because I'm realizing that every history teacher I ever had was right; we need to learn from our past so we can try to avoid making those same mistakes in the future.§ I also bring it up because everything I just told you is super confusing and vague. If you were to sit down and read all of the information about the case, you'll see that the court stops short of defining exactly what a "true threat" is. It's because there is a lot to take into consideration when defining what is and isn't a threat.

The case of Robert Watts was long before the world of the Internet and social networking were even part of the equation. When you look at the case of Justin Carter, it's difficult to infer inflection and intent through written text. Think about how you are reading this text right now. If you have been to one of my workshops before or you happen to know me in real life, there's a chance it's my voice in your head and you can take a pretty good guess what this would all sound like if I were sitting there reading this to you. If we've never met before, there's a good chance the Charlie Brown adult "womp womp" voice is in there teaching you about supreme court cases.

---

§ See Mr. Mintz, I was paying attention!

Or Morgan Freeman, which would be awesome.

CRIMES INVOLVING SPEECH:

Also not covered under the First Amendment are any forms of speech that are used to commit a crime. The big three examples of this are perjury, extortion, and harassment. For the purposes of this text, we're just going to be looking at harassment as the primary example of this particular exception.

Harassment is a very broad term, and can refer to a wide variety of behaviors that can be subject to both criminal and civil liability. Civil, being private disputes between persons or organizations; criminal involves actions that are considered to be harmful to society as a whole. The laws, definitions and punishments surrounding criminal harassment vary state by state. Much like with threats, there is a lot to take into consideration with these cases, and because it is defined on the state level, the treatment of similar cases may look a lot different depending on where you are.

Harassment (or in some cases, bullying) can be considered a crime and actually folds into both of the exceptions I've already talked about. In 2017, a woman in Spokane, Washington who found herself facing multiple counts of malicious harassment after yelling racially-motivated comments to her neighbors.

A First Amendment lawyer, David Bodney, was consulted in a news article pertaining to the case and cited incitement, fighting words, and true threat in his explanation of exceptions to freedom of speech.[23] Repeated violent language and actions towards another person can constitute harassment, and therefore is not protected by freedom of speech, as defined by the exceptions we've discussed.

If your head is spinning right now, don't worry; mine too. This is a lot to take in, especially since it can be really confusing. More so when you start to look at the differences between state and federal laws. We are going to talk more about bullying and harassment in another chapter, so I'll let you take a break from all this legal talk, for now.

WHAT JUST HAPPENED?

Not even going to lie to you, writing all of that was strangely enjoyable, but now my brain hurts and there's a good chance yours does as well. That was a whole lot of information crammed into a chapter, but I can bet that your reaction to some, if not all, of that was, "Wow! I did not know that." Actually, part of the reason this was so enjoyable to me was the fact that there is so much that I can't get out or say during a workshop because of time restraints. While I do address the whole idea of freedom of speech and the Internet, I can't go into this much depth.

Believe it or not, information like this is important to know, especially if you're someone who wants to make the First Amendment argument. Really, any argument. So often lately, when you see people arguing online or in the real world, they have only surface knowledge of what they are arguing about. So yes, we understand the First Amendment grants us freedom of speech and expression, but do we fully comprehend what that all actually means? Hopefully now you have a better idea and *that*, my friends, is why I took the time to make sure that we covered it.

Sure, none of that is going to make for very interesting conversation at a party, but you never know. I've, personally, gone on long rants about the mating and communication habits of lobsters at a party. I'm also just a little bit odd so that might have something to do with it. But if you are curious to know more, I suggest picking up The Secret Lives of Lobsters by Trevor Corson. I don't know Trevor and I'm not getting paid to promote his book; I just genuinely find it fascinating.

That all said, I did just offload a bunch of information into your brains so if you feel the need to take a break from reading this book, I don't blame you. To offer further proof that I am a fan of the Internet, I actually finished writing the main part of this chapter and allowed myself a small break to watch some of P!NK's past performances on YouTube. Then I ended up watching Doctor Mike. Followed by *Honest Trailers*. Honestly, it's all a vicious cycle.

JOSH GUNDERSON

just kidding doesn't cut it in the online world

Did you know there was an actual Humor Research Lab in the United States? This wasn't how I was planning to start this chapter, but for the sake of argument let's just all roll with it because we're learning something new. I was casually searching what the most sarcastic state in the US was and ended up reading a 12-page document breaking down the funniest cities in the US. For the record, Chicago, IL came in first, with Boston, MA in second.[24] My current home of Orlando, FL doesn't appear anywhere in the document which is a crime because some of the funniest people I know live and work here so I'm sensing there may be some flaws in the research done here.

My point, and I do have one, is that if you've ever been to one of my workshops or presentations, then you know that they are full of humor because that is my chosen form of communication. Also, it's been proven that using humor can actually improve retention in students of any age.[25] My argument is that when an audience is having a good time, they are going to remember the things that entertained them more than the bits that were boring them out of their minds. So I'm pretty much an education ninja because I'm sneaking the learning into each and every joke.

One of the big things I am always sure to touch on in any workshop is the idea of "just kidding" when it comes to the online world. When I'm hanging out with my friends and joking around, it's a lot different than when we're chatting in the online world. If my friend Kevin is about to make a stupid joke that we both know I'm going to hate, I may say something along the lines of, "I will end you." In that moment, face-to-face, I know I'm kidding and he knows I'm kidding. But what if I post that same comment on his Instagram? Or Facebook? I know I'm kidding; he knows I'm kidding, but does the rest of the world know I'm kidding?

Think about Justin Carter. He posted something in the heat of the moment and, according to some reports, had also posted "LOL, JK"[26] following his threatening statement. That didn't stop him from losing five years of his life to that Facebook post. Just kidding just doesn't work.

That's the important difference when it comes to the online world. In real life, you can hear my voice, you can see my face, and you can likely tell that I'm kidding. Remember Robert Watts? The context of his statement is what saved him; people that were there when it happened could testify to his intent. When it comes to a text message or online comment, that context just isn't there. That tone and inflection are lost in the robotic words on a screen.

In April, 2014, a Dutch teenager learned her lesson about attempting to joke around on the Internet when she took the idea of "just kidding around" to an extreme on Twitter. The young girl only identified as "Sarah" posted on her Twitter account a tweet directed at American Airlines that read, "hello my name's Ibrahim and I'm from Afghanistan. I'm part of Al Qaida and on June 1st I'm gonna do something really big bye."

American Airlines social media was quick to respond with, "we take these threats very seriously.

Your IP address and details will be forwarded to security and the FBI."

"Sarah" proceeded to have something of a meltdown following the airline's tweet, blasting out, "OMFG I was kidding," "I'm so sorry I'm scared now," and "I was just kidding pls don't I'm just a girl pls."

Just 24 hours after posting the tweet, "Sarah" turned herself in to the authorities where she was charged with "posting a false or alarming announcement" and spent several hours being questioned by investigators before being released.[27] [28]

Ultimately, charges against the teenager were dropped once no credible threat was found from the investigation. Many felt that the airline's actions were over the top when it came to dealing with the threatening tweet, but think of all of that from a real world perspective. What if American Airlines decided, "Oh she's just a kid joking around? Well, no problem then!" and then come June 1st, something horrific happened?

They have a responsibility to their customers and employees to ensure they are safe when flying their airline. As someone who spends an obscene amount of time flying, I appreciate their commitment to safety and taking threats like that seriously. It's the same if a threat is made at your school or place of work.

Once again, this may seem like an over-the-top example, but it's the reality of the digital world that we live in. It can be very easy to forget there is a world be-yond the screen and that your actions online can have very real world impacts even if you are just kidding around. Your actions can see you banned from a social media platform, fired from your job, or even arrested. No one needs or wants that kind of headache.

This is proof positive why it's important to really slow ourselves down and take the time to think while we're online. I do this constantly! Like I said, I am a very jokey person, but when I'm responding to things online or posting my own thoughts out on Twitter, I'm constantly thinking to myself "How is this going to be interpreted online?" Will my friends know I'm joking? Will a random person who found my comments know I'm joking? If the answer is unclear or a straight up "no" then I refrain from commenting because it's not worth the risk. Maybe I'll just wait until I see them face to face.

JOSH GUNDERSON

yes, you can be fired for that tweet

We have gotten far too used at how quickly we are able to project whatever we are thinking out into the world, and it's causing a lot of problems. I'm not just talking to the teenagers either! Adults are just as guilty of sticking their feet in their mouths in the online world. People I know personally have lost their jobs because of tweets, Facebook status updates, TikTok videos, and more. Even celebrities are not immune from losing work due to inappropriate or controversial tweets.

Stars like Gina Carano, Jake Paul, and Roseanne Barr all found themselves on the chopping block from their acting jobs after social media posts blew up in their faces.[29] Granted, all three of them worked either directly for, or some subsidiary of, the Disney Company who is known for their rigid standards for employee conduct. There is definitely still a lesson to be learned from their firings for all us normal people.

It makes sense when something a celebrity does wrong goes viral because of their notoriety and massive followings, but someone with just one hundred followers and zero fame can get themselves into the same amount of trouble. That lesson was learned in the worst way possible by a public relations executive named Justine Sacco. Prior to taking off on her 11-hour flight to South Africa, Sacco tweeted out to her 170 followers, "Going to Africa. Hope I don't get AIDS. Just kidding. I'm white!"[30]

While in the air, with her phone unable to receive any communications, the tweet went viral, catching the attention of the world and sparking a trending hashtag of #HasJustineLandedYet. She deleted the tweet and her entire account soon after landing at her destination, but at that point, the damage was done. She was subsequently let go from the company where she worked. Despite the fact that she deleted the tweet and her account, it doesn't stop it from living on the Internet forever.

Do a quick Google search for her name and you'll find dozens of articles, screenshots and information about the infamous tweet. Think about what kind of damage that could do to her career in the future. A recent survey found that 90% of employers factor an applicant's social media profiles and activities into their hiring decisions with about 79% of them rejecting a candidate based on their social media accounts.[31]

Back in 2015 a Texan teen, "Cella," lost her job before she even started after posting a derogatory tweet in reference to her new gig at a Jet's Pizza franchise. In a since-deleted tweet she complained "Ew I start this f*ck *ss job tomorrow" followed by some thumbs down emojis. The manager was alerted to the tweet by another employee and responded with "no you don't start this FA job today! I just fired you! Good luck with your no money, no job life!"[32] Admittedly, not the most professional actions from either party but it's the price you pay when you don't slow down and think before you post.

In this case we're not only looking at somebody's personal brand, but a professional one as well. While the Internet might have rallied behind "Cella," the professional world might not be so kind as she has established herself as being unprofessional. That doesn't mean the independent owner of the Jet's Pizza franchise, Robert Waple, was in the right. His actions were just as unprofessional. The parent company that owns the Jet's name issued a statement clarifying that the location in question was independently owned and operated (effectively distancing themselves from the action) and they regretted the behavior of both parties involved.[33]

More recently, a barista at a Starbucks in Los Angeles was fired after sharing a customer's crazy order via social media. The barista in question, Josie Morales, posted on twitter a photo of a drink and the label depicting the instructions on his Twitter account along with the caption, "On today's episode of why I want to quit my job." Morales was fired after the post went viral for violating Starbucks social media policy.[34]

I know I'm sounding like a broken record when I say this, but our actions in the online world have real world consequences. We feel very safe when it's just the screen in front of us, but every time we hit that enter button, we are sending ourselves out for others to see. Just because we turn off the computer or put down the phone, doesn't make it all go away. The world is still out there and it is watching.

As I mentioned before, your social media profiles are being used as a reference to what kind of person you are. Are you the type of individual a company wants working for them? The same applies to colleges. According to a survey conducted by Kaplan, 36% of college admissions officers have visited an applicant's social media profile and have used what they found there as part of their determination.[35] How are they finding you? By searching Google! It's really that simple.

In the last 10 years that I have been working in education, online safety, and bullying prevention, I have been contracted by companies and schools to help train people how to search for information about applicants through social media. Often, the work has been outsourced to me to help them run social media background checks on people because they don't have the people or the resources to do so themselves. Not only are those reports and studies proving to us that this is more of a reality, I'm here to tell you for certain that it's happening.

Some people like to argue these kinds of searches are a violation of privacy and are shocked to learn that it isn't. Part of the reason is that a lot of our laws have not caught up with changes in technology. If you have public profiles, accounts, or blogs, those are all fair game for a current or potential employer to look at. Keep that in mind as you are posting, and be sure to take the time to look over your profiles and accounts should you find yourself in a position where you know you'll have people looking for you online.

what's on your social media resume?

Hopefully by now you're wondering exactly what it is these recruiters and employers are looking for when they are searching for you online. I can't speak to what others are looking for when it comes to checking out what I like to call your "social media resume," but I can tell you what I keep my eyes peeled for when I'm doing the legwork for others. Sometimes I am given very specific things to keep an eye out for and other times it's left to my discretion. So I go into each of these searches with one simple thought on my mind: would I want this person working for *me*?

If you're wondering when is the right time to start thinking about your digital resume, the answer is right this very moment. Everything we do online leaves behind digital breadcrumbs that lead right back to us, so you always want to be thinking about where that trail leads and what kind of impression you are leaving with someone. More importantly, there's a good chance that what they find online is their first impression of you.

When I was in college, I was the assistant manager of a small grocery store. My responsibilities included overseeing and hiring for the front end operations (cashiers, etc). A large majority of applicants were high school students, either from the town where the store was located or the next town over. You better believe that I did a search online for each and every one of those applicants and some of them ended up in the "no hire" pile as a result of those searches.

So what am I looking for? Let's take a look!

PROFILE PICTURES:

Think of your profile picture as the new official first impression a person has of you. What am I looking at? Some of the things I've seen have included teenagers holding bottles of alcohol looking like they were more than just holding the bottle, my potential candidate flipping off the camera, or, in place of an actual photo, an inappropriate meme.

As you are getting ready to job hunt or apply to colleges, that would be a great time to change up your profile photo to something a bit more professional. I always think to myself, "if I go missing, this is the picture they are going to use on the news." So I keep it looking good, no one wants a bad picture on the side of a milk carton!

As you move into the professional world, pre- or post-college, and join sites along the lines of LinkedIn, you want to make sure that you are not only keeping that resume updated, but also taking a good look at your profile photo. Here are some things that employers really don't want to see on your profiles, especially on sites like LinkedIn. This list is 100% based on things I've seen over the years and it's just as cringe-worthy as you can imagine:

- Selfies, bathroom mirrors especially. Just don't do it!
- A group photo. Why? Because I have no idea which person is you.
- A photo taken of you at a party.
- A lewd photo of you partially undressed or inappropriately dressed.

- A photo of you holding a beer (think backyard BBQ photos).

I am lucky enough to have friends who are amazingly talented photographers, and are willing to have some fun going around and taking photos of me. We may not all be so lucky, but with the quality of cell phone cameras these days, it wouldn't be hard to head out with a friend and take some professional headshots.

Keep in mind that professional doesn't have to mean boring! Don't be afraid to have a little fun with them and show off who you are and your personality. Just be sure to keep professionalism in mind as you do so. Once you have a good selection of pictures, sit down with some friends or even an advisor and pick which photos put the best foot forward. Pick one for each of your social media profiles to give them a bit of variety!

ABOUT ME:

What you put in your mini social media biographies matters! I want to know if the person in your cover letter is the same person I'm finding on social media. Remember that even with private profiles, bios are usually still public and can be seen by anyone. Not only are we looking at the contents of these "about me" sections, we're taking a good look at proper spelling and grammar as an indication of how seriously you take those skills.

Remember, you are your brand, so take charge of the message that you are putting forward. Even simply bullet-pointing what you are interested in or the talents you would like to highlight. You usually don't have a lot of room in these bios, so make sure that you are using it wisely and putting your best foot forward.

Thinking back to your privacy, make sure you aren't revealing too much personal information in your bios. Avoiding putting where you go to school, messaging app usernames, and phone numbers (all things I've seen in social media bios of high school students). Remember those digital breadcrumbs? Don't leave a path to more social media for someone to potentially take a look at!

YOUR FRIENDS:

When it comes to the world of social media, your friends become something of an unofficial reference for you. When I'm taking a look at a candidate's profile, I'm not just looking at what they post, I'm looking at what their friends are posting. That's not to say I'm clicking through all of your friends and looking at their timelines; I'm looking at what they are posting to your page or what kind of comments they are leaving and how you react to them.

The best thing to do is ask friends not to tag you in inappropriate photos or memes that may be considered uncouth by an employer or college admissions officer. Remember, not everyone has the same sense of humor and you may be projecting the wrong message. If your friends leave a comment on a status or photo that may be inappropriate, delete it. Should they upload an unflattering photo of you, ask them to remove it. Even if you are not the one posting or tagging, it could still be seen and cast you in a poor light.

Don't be afraid to have these conversations as they may save you a lot of headache in the future, and it will keep potential employers from seeing things you may not want to be associated with. An awkward conversation now with a friend can save you from an even more awkward conversation during a job interview. Ask your friends to be respectful of your image and brand when they are posting on your timelines or tagging you in posts.

PICTURES:

This one is probably a given, but it is a good tie-in to everything I just discussed. Make sure the photos of you that both you and your friends are posting represent you in the best light. I'm not saying you can't have a social life and share it with your friends and family, but find the delicate balance that exists.

My example? I am well over 21-years-old. By definition I am an adult and I'm free to enjoy adult things. While I'm not a big party person, I am known for joining my friends for a drink every now and again and I'm a huge fan of cruises. I am an experienced bartender and enjoy the fine art of mixology. These are all things that I am happy to share on my Instagram feed because they are what I enjoy. However, I am sure to be smart about them.

When I am out with my friends and having fun, I'm very cognizant of when photos are being taken. I'm not going to say there are no photos of me with alcohol anywhere on the Internet, there are, but are they wild party photos? Absolutely not. If a friend does happen to snap a picture of me, I'm sure to ask to see it and, if it's something I don't want out on the web, I'll ask that they delete it. Should they catch a candid photo that I don't know about and it gets posted, I'll ask that it be removed.

Sometimes it's a bit awkward, but at this point all of my friends are used to it and I promise yours will be understanding. We're all human and we like to have fun, but we also want to be seen in the best light possible, especially in the digital world. Start training yourself to think of these things now! I completely understand that it seems weird, but we are living in a time when some people have an online presence that begins from the moment they are born and will continue through the rest of their lives!

USERNAMES AND EMAILS:

Applying for jobs today looks a whole lot different from when I was a teenager. Remember that grocery store job I had? I started there when I was 15 years old and the application process was me walking into the store, identifying the manager and telling him I wanted a job. I filled out a very simple paper application and handed it to him. Today, that process is a lot different as most places, outside of maybe some small mom and pop businesses, are using the Internet to find applicants.**

A key component to communication today, especially with online applications, is the email address. Odds are, that is what will be used to contact you to schedule an interview and will be used for delivering information relevant to the process. As a result, you should make sure that your email address is the best representation of you.

** I actually want to make a funny note. I went to my old grocery store job's website and found that in order to apply you are now downloading that (almost) same paper application as a PDF to fill out and email back to the respective store manager. Given that this is a small, family-owned chain, it tracks. And it's honestly adorably endearing to me. I might just be old and nostalgic.

I am a major proponent of creating a safe email address when you are first getting into the online world, choosing email addresses and usernames that don't reveal any personal information including your name, where you live, or where you go to school. As you get ready to apply for colleges and jobs, that's the time to create your professional email with something as simple as your name and begin the transition to using that full time.

Why? Well, here's just a handful of the colorful email addresses that I have seen on job applications over the past few years:

- Ho4Sho@emailaddress.com
- gamerfreak365@emailaddress.com
- baller4lfe@emailaddress.com
- fatbootiecutie69@emailaddress.com
- kiloofcoke420@emailaddress.com
- drunkgurl467@emailaddress.com
- beastlyjohnson@emailaddress.com

Now, some of these examples are pretty obvious as to why you wouldn't want to throw them onto a job or college application. A couple may make you scratch your head and wonder what the problem is.

I'll use the example of "gamerfreak365." While it's not inherently bad by any stretch of the imagination, you want to think about the image you are portraying to a potential employer. Granted, if you are applying to a video game company they may not bat an eye, but you likely aren't making the best impression for an internship at a marketing agency or a job that requires government clearance.[††]

WHAT YOU'RE POSTING ABOUT:

We all have bad days at work; it happens. I've even been known to have a rough day here and there when working with schools. Once I drove all the way from Boston to southern New Jersey for a speaking engagement to learn that the organization that hired me never passed along to the school that I was going to be visiting for some workshops. I was met by a sea of confused faces and found myself pretty annoyed. I've arrived at venues to find them unprepared and scrambling, making for some uncomfortable moments for me. One time I asked if they had gotten water for me and was met with, "Oh, we thought that was a joke."

Imagine that I decided I was annoyed enough to rant about it on social media. I call out the unprofessionalism and the poor welcome I received. I feel good because I got it off my chest and my friends and followers get a good chuckle at my misfortune.

[††] For the record, "gamerfreak365" was applying to one of the examples I gave and didn't not receive the opportunity to interview.

Now imagine that you are a school administrator or a conference planner looking into booking me for an engagement. You check out my website and like what you see, but then you click over to my Twitter and see me bad mouthing another organization. Much like "just kidding" you might not be getting the full context of the situation, and you just see me acting like a jerk and a bit of a diva. I'm probably not getting a phone call or email from you about a job.

The same goes for you when it comes to what you are putting online. Are you bad mouthing and complaining constantly about your current job? Are you posting nasty things about your teachers? Are you always posting negative things and generally complaining about life? These are the things we are looking for in your posts, and often it speaks volumes about your personality. How would that look when transferred into a workplace? Is that the type of person they want in the office?

I completely understand that life happens and sometimes it's not the greatest. When I sit down and look back at my Tweets and Facebook posts spanning most of 2020, things were pretty dire. There were plenty of unpleasant feelings towards a lot of what was happening in the world with unemployment, the presidential election, the storming of the Capitol building, etc. And yes, I commented on all of it along the way.

But I also made sure there was a balance and that my timelines were not all doom and gloom. If you are on Twitter doing nothing but starting or participating in arguments with others, it's not the best look.

ON THE JOB:

If you look back at any of the stories in the previous chapter, you'll remember that you're not in the clear once you've landed the job. Be sure to take the time to read your company's employee handbook because there's a good chance there is a social media policy in place that explains what is and is not acceptable to post about when it comes to your job. I know that an employee handbook isn't exactly a thrilling read, but do yourself the favor and look through it for those policies. Ignorance of their existence is not an excuse.

The truth of the matter is many companies will continue to monitor their employees on social media. A prime example of this is the Walt Disney Company which consistently keeps an eye on what is being posted about them, especially by their cast members. I have known quite a few people who have been terminated by the company for posting backstage photos, posting things that represent the company in a negative light, or conduct that goes against the values and ideals of the company.

Again, sometimes this work is outsourced, and they will ask third parties like myself to look into their employees' conduct in the online world. Like you need to work to protect your personal brand, they are looking out for theirs. If a known employee is acting in such a way that may reflect poorly on the company, there's a good chance they will lose their job as a result of their actions. I'm not saying it's always fair, remember, we're all still catching up with technology and some are more behind than others.

A prime example is Brittany Tomlinson, aka Kombucha Girl, who went viral after trying the fizzy drink for the first time. Shortly after the video went viral, she was terminated from her job at a Texas bank, the management fearing her online presence could be a liability for the establishment.[36] She has since landed on her feet thanks to that same viral video, but this isn't always the case for everyone.

JOSH GUNDERSON

the internet is forever
(kind of)

Every time I take a screenshot on my new phone, I feel like the world's worst Jedi. All I need to do is, very carefully, wave my hand over the screen in a specific way and whatever I'm looking at will be captured. It's the same hand motion I use when walking through automatic doors at Target. World's. Worst. Jedi.

That's all it takes now to capture a moment on my phone: the wave of my hand. In an effort to sound old, back in my day when I wanted to screenshot something, it involved a very intricate pushing of buttons on the phone and when done incorrectly, you turned your phone off. The early 2000's were a seriously dark time. There were dragons.

Remember that new phone I told you I just got? I just discovered that it allows me to make screen recordings! I'm now able to turn on the little recorder and capture videos of what I'm looking at or even create "how to" videos involving apps. This is very exciting to me because it enhances how I can discuss app safety for parents and how to adjust settings. It's really the simple things that make you happy as you get older.

I bring this up for the simple fact that it has become easier for us to capture things that we see online. I will admit that it's a bit of conjecture for anyone to say that what goes on the Internet stays there forever. This is a tactic I have used in front of many audiences to drive home a point, and while it's not a lie, it's not the truth.

I think BBC's Simon Platt said it best in an article for OneZero: "When we put something online, it becomes a sort of Schrödinger's cat: simultaneously deleted and undeletable. We have to assume it could be deleted at any time, but also that it could exist forever, a hydra of mortifying photos and embarrassing status updates from the past. There might be traces of it that someone could follow to recover. Deleted tweets resurface again, not in their original form, but as pixelated JPEGed screenshots. Online information is permanent—less like a museum exhibition and more like a stain on a favorite T-shirt."[37]

The perceived permanence of the Internet is something I am constantly keeping in mind whenever I post and you should as well. The number of times I have typed something out only to delete it probably numbers somewhere in the thousands at this point because I like to do something of a spot check about how I'm feeling at that moment. Am I ranting? Am I sharing too much information? Do I just need a Snickers? If I'm in a particularly snarky mood, I'll stop and do a 10-count before I consider hitting the enter button and usually I'll end up deleting whatever I wrote and moving on with my life.

Was I always like this? Absolutely not. For example, I joined Twitter in June of 2009, well over a decade ago. Since my joining date, I have posted over 13,000 tweets. There's a good chance that somewhere in all those years, I said something stupid and regrettable. Perhaps I thought I was being funny and provocative? Perhaps I was probably hoping for all the likes and retweets I would need to become Internet-famous. Who knows.

It's important to keep this in mind as you begin to grow and develop your own digital identity. As someone who has worked around teenagers for the better part of his career, I understand how, as you grow, your opinions and feelings on certain topics can change over time. As you get older and perhaps move away from the views of the adults in your life and begin to forge your own view of the world, the person you are may not be so fond of the person you were. I can say I definitely feel this way about myself. I definitely have said things for the sake of being provocative that could easily ruin people's views of me. I'm not proud of that person, and I'm sure glad he has grown up.

Within the past few years we have seen the past catching up with people in the form of tweets that were posted for the sake of making an off-color joke and being provocative. In 2018, director James Gunn and comedian Kevin Hart came under fire in separate incidents for their past online posts. As a result, Gunn was fired by Marvel and Hart was dropped from hosting the 2019 Academy Awards.

I bring these two up specifically for a couple reasons. The first is that if you go back and look at their Twitter accounts, the offending tweets were deleted from their respective timelines. This means nothing in the world of the Internet because if I do a quick Google search of their names with "tweets," I'm met with a number of articles written about the incidents as well as screenshots of those tweets. Matter of fact, look at any of the stories I've shared in previous chapters and search for them; their status updates and tweets will live on in the form of screenshots.

The second reason I bring up Gunn and Hart is because of how the two men reacted to the dug up tweets and resulting fall-out. Hart was asked to issue a formal apology by the Academy of Motion Picture Arts and Sciences who sponsor the Oscars. Hart declined, saying, "I'd never apologize for what was never intended to be disrespectful — I'd never allow the public to win for something I know wasn't malicious."[38] Now is the time to think back on the intent and impact of joking around in the online world. I will note that Hart did eventually issue an apology for his past actions, but by that point the damage was done and the outcry from the LGBTQ+ community for what they felt to be an insincere apology led to him officially walking away from the hosting job.

Gunn, on the other hand, took to heart his firing from the family-friendly Marvel Studios and used the opportunity to self-reflect and blamed no one but himself for the termination. Unlike Hart, Gunn did not lash out at the studio or those who were calling for his being removed from the *Guardians of the Galaxy* franchise and issued a thoughtful and honest apology for his past behavior. His ability to look back, reflect, learn and grow were potentially all factors in his being

brought back by Marvel a year after the tweets resur-
faced.[39]

Please do not read this as my saying you can apologize your way out of anything and make it all okay.
I'm not. I bring this up to point out that there is some
permanence to what you put on the Internet so it's important to take the time to think before you hit that enter button. But, we're all human; we make mistakes. If
you do make a mistake, it's all a part of being alive.
Obviously, mistakes within reason. Be willing to learn,
to educate yourself, and evolve. Showing your ability
to grow from mistakes goes a lot further than doubling
down on your words and working in vain to defend
them.

Now is about the time that you might be thinking,
"But Josh, what about all those disappearing apps?
Snapchats will disappear after you look at them and
then they're gone! Right?"

Wrong!

Don't feel bad. You wouldn't be the first person to
bring up apps like Snapchat in an effort to prove that
things disappear from the Internet. Unfortunately, that
was found not to be the case with the popular app. As
a matter of fact, Snapchat found itself in hot water with
the Federal Trade Commission (FTC) when it was
found that the app's claim that pictures sent with the
app "disappear" was far from the truth.

According to the complaint, Snapchat misrepresented its product on multiple counts to the consumer downloading the app. Here's a tidbit from the FTC's official press release following the hearings on the complaints brought against Snapchat:

Snapchat, the developer of a popular mobile messaging app, has agreed to settle Federal Trade Commission charges that it deceived consumers with promises about the disappearing nature of messages sent through the service. The FTC case also alleged that the company deceived consumers over the amount of personal data it collected and the security measures taken to protect that data from misuse and unauthorized disclosure. In fact, the case alleges, Snapchat's failure to secure its Find Friends feature resulted in a security breach that enabled attackers to compile a database of 4.6 million Snapchat usernames and phone numbers.[40]

This case is actually the reason why you receive a notification should the recipient of your snap decide to screenshot or screen record what you sent them. Believe it or not, we didn't have that feature when the app was first launched. Why they haven't evolved to stop screenshots from being taken all together is beyond me. The technology exists, and I know this because for some weird reason Snapchat hasn't implemented it. If, for some weird reason, ShopDisney can stop me from screenshotting a picture of a Lilo & Stitch hoodie I want, they can prevent people from screenshotting the weird cat videos I send them.

Sadly, even with this notification feature, there's no stopping the countless apps that are available that allow users to recover or capture snaps without a notification being sent to the originator of the content. A quick Google search will reveal over half a million articles and videos showing you how to do just that. I'm not telling this to make you paranoid, but you may want to reconsider what you are sending. There's a chance Fox Mulder was onto something when he said "Trust No One."

Additionally, those pictures are still hanging out on Snapchat's servers most of the time. Remember, *everything* we do online leaves behind those digital breadcrumbs and sending something off to one of your friends isn't as simple as that message going from Point A to Point B. There's a bit of a journey it has to go on first and, in the case of Snapchat, that journey involves a layover on the company's servers where unopened snaps are stored for a period of 30 days if the recipient doesn't open them. There have also been instances where Snapchat has handed over unopened snaps to law enforcement when issued a warrant for them.[41]

Then there was the event known as "The Snappening" where over 200,000 nude images sent by

Snapchat users were leaked onto the Internet via a massive data dump. Reports point towards third party apps designed to capture snaps as the cause of the stolen images.[42]

All of this is good food for thought the next time you are doing anything online. Big Brother might not always be watching, but someone is. Unfortunately there are some not-so-great people out there in the world that enjoy causing trouble for others. The key is to be mindful about everything you are sending out into the world, and remain vigilant about what kind of digital breadcrumbs you are leaving behind. Before you hit that enter button ask yourself, is this really worth it?

the chapter about sexting

If you ever find yourself craving some *Real House-wives*-style drama complete with backstabbing and name-calling, I suggest you look into the sordid history of the Snapchat company now known as Snap, Inc. There's also the idea that drove the creation of the app which, put very simply, was "girls would be more like-ly to send me racy photos if they disappeared."[43] From that simple thought, three Stanford University students set to work on creating what would eventually become Snapchat.

While the concept and practice of sexting didn't start with Snapchat, it was surely exacerbated by the app as it gave users a false sense of security when it came to their inappropriate photos. If you feel like diving into the history of sending inappropriate messages, it actually dates back to 30,000 B.C. with Paleolithic cave paintings depicting various sexual acts by humans and animals. In 1150 A.D. carrier pigeons were known to deliver a spicy message now and then, with the downside being the six-month wait between messages. Irish novelist James Joyce was known to write quite saucy letters to his wife and the invention of the instant camera in 1948 was a game changer when it came to photography. As you can see, the concept isn't new, but the methods have evolved over the years.

The term "sext" didn't enter our vernacular until 2004 when a Canadian newspaper used it in an article about the alleged inappropriate texts between David Beckham and his then-assistant Rebecca Loos.[44] At this time cell phone cameras were about two years old and you probably would have been better off with the carrier pigeons at that stage in the game. Again, dark times.

As the cell-phone camera technology became more advanced, so did the problems that they created, especially when it came to the concept of sexting. There have been a multitude of high-profile cases of sexting between adults including Brett Favre, Tiger Woods and Anthony Weiner. While embarrassing and potentially career damaging, these messages were exchanged between adults. In many cases we are seeing these same types of messages occurring between underage teens, causing a mountain of trouble and felony charges.

One of the biggest questions I get on this topic from students and parents alike is what the laws are surrounding this issue. The problem is that there is no straightforward answer to this. Sexting laws are a relatively new concept in the legal world, and some places have some catching up to do. You'll be surprised to learn that when it comes to laws surrounding sexting, it's up to each individual state to create and enact their laws. As of this writing, only 26 of the 50 states have some sort of law on the books when it comes to sexting. When it comes to sexting involving individuals under the age of 18, many states are looking to the federal laws surrounding child pornography, which comes with very strict consequences for perpetrators up to and including prison time.

Again, we find ourselves in very complicated territory because a lot of these laws were written at a time when we weren't all carrying a high-definition camera in our back pocket. As a result, we are seeing 16-year-olds being charged with manufacturing and distribution of child pornography and facing 10+ years in prison. If the image or content crosses state lines (which can easily happen in this digital world), federal laws regarding child pornography come into play.

So what can you do to protect yourself? The first, and most obvious, answer to this is never take or share explicit or suggestive photos. If it doesn't exist, then it can't get into the wrong hands or be shared all over the Internet. Just like I ask you to take the time to think before you post, I'm going to ask you to think before you snap. I'm not just talking about Snapchat, I'm talking about any picture you take. Even if you never send it off from your phone, if it is discovered there is still potential for charges including the manufacturing and possession of child pornography.

Remember when it comes to apps that promise messages disappear, there are always ways around it from specialty apps to simply taking a screenshot. Keep in mind that when you're sending these messages, it isn't as simple as going from point A to point B. It's traveling through your network provider's servers as well as those of the app you are using. We're always leaving behind those little digital breadcrumbs with every little thing that we do. Don't ever forget that!

Sometimes receiving these types of messages is beyond our control, so what should you do? If you find yourself on the receiving end of an explicit image or video, delete it immediately. While there is no stopping from someone sending you these images, you can control how it will affect you. Because of this, many sexting laws prohibit "receiving and keeping" explicit images. Therefore, you are only in violation of the law if you choose to hold on to the image.

If possible, reach out to the sender and ask them to stop sending you these kinds of messages. Explain the trouble the both of you could get into, should these images end up in the public view. Additionally, reach out to a trusted adult and let them in on what is happening and allow them to help you. Be honest in what you tell them so they can figure out the best way to support you. Remember, we're all human and make mistakes. Much of the time it's better to own up to it sooner rather than later, before it becomes a bigger issue down the line.

It's also important to never forward or share these types of images to others, should you be on the receiving end of them. In addition to charges of possession, you're also looking are distribution of child pornography. Each person you forward that image to becomes another count of that charge and those people will be looking at possession charges for themselves. With how quickly messages can be shared and the reach we have with technology, it's very easy for an issue like sexting to snowball into a big problem for everyone involved.

This is also a great time to remind you to be mindful of your surroundings when taking photos. We've talked about revealing too much information, but what about revealing too much of you or someone else? It's happened!

I was working with a school district in Ohio when an administrator shared a story of unintentional sexting that occured within the high school. A young woman was in the locker room with her team following a field hockey practice when she snapped a selfie in the mirror of the bathroom. When she posted the photo, she was unaware of one of her teammates, topless in the reflection of the mirror. She found herself in a lot of hot water for the image, but the incident was contained and dealt with in a timely manner and she did not end up facing charges. The post was removed, but that's never a guarantee that it's gone. It just takes one person taking a screenshot.

friends, followers, and fame

"How do I become famous?"

This is a legitimate question I have received on more than one occasion while working with students. It has come from seniors in high school, middle schoolers and even elementary school students. The reason is that the Internet has created a different breed of celebrity in the form of content creators online. Even big name celebrities got their start creating content on social media: Justin Beiber, Shawn Mendes, Tori Kelly and Charlie Puth, to name a few. As a result, we see more and more people striving to find that same level of notoriety from their social accounts, praying they go viral.

I never have advice on how to make this happen, mostly because I have no idea. That and the concept of fame and virality is really subjective and requires more of a deeper philosophical conversation than I am willing to offer up right now. Have I gone viral before? I have. Do I know why it happened? I haven't the slightest clue. Have I been able to recreate that level of success? Not on purpose. What's it like to have something go viral? Honestly, it's kind of annoying and really kills your phone battery from the notifications.

When people ask me about becoming Internet famous, my mind goes to the movie *He's Just Not That Into You*. If you've never seen it, I'm pretty certain it's on Netflix so this is a good time to take a break and give it a watch. Grab your parents and have a family movie night. It's a great ensemble film and it's PG-13 so if you're old enough to be on social media, you're old enough to sit down and watch this movie.

Yes, I know the movie is about dating, but some of it actually applies to what I'm talking about. There's a great scene between Justin Long and Ginnifer Goodwin where they talk about exceptions and rules when it comes to dating. Long's character tells Goodwin that the guy she is at this bar looking for is never going to call her because he's not interested. She goes on a bit of a tirade about why it could still happen because a friend of a friend had it work out for her. Long points out this makes her the exception and Goodwin's character is the rule.

The clip is actually on YouTube but, honestly, just hunt down and watch the movie. It's a good time. You'll laugh, you'll cry, you'll audibly gasp at one point. Everyone's having fun. Well, not everyone but it's a rom-com; someone has to have a bad day. Those are the rules. (See what I did there).

The same logic applies to the idea of Internet fame. All those YouTubers, TikTokers, Twitterers, and Twitchers are the exception. Many of us are the rule. I'm including myself in that, I am the rule! I've had a few of my blog posts gain some attention here and there and nothing has come out of it. I had a tweet that garnered just shy of 1 million impressions in under 24 hours and I'm still sitting here in my one-bedroom apartment wondering if Honda will take a pint of blood as a payment this month. I am the rule, not the exception.

I bring all of this up because the constant desire for fame that I am seeing makes me worried about what social media is doing to us mentally, emotionally and psychologically. It's important to remember, when it comes to social media, what we are seeing is polished perfection, and often it's an expensive lie.

One woman learned that the hard way when she put herself into debt while attempting to become an Instagram-famous influencer. Lissette Caleiro would spend hundreds of dollars every month to ensure that her followers never saw her in the same outfit twice on her feed and was splurging constantly on trips and meals out. All for the perfect Instagram post. Reality slapped hard when she found herself $10,000 in the hole for the sake of gaining Internet fame.[45]

Fame is a common desire and has been since the dawn of time, I'm sure. Our perception of it has changed over the years and now we look at follower counts and "likes" as a metric for what it means to be famous. Remember my viral tweet? It has over 20,000 likes and was retweeted almost 3,000 times. Want to know how much money I made from that tweet? Nothing. Any new followers? Nope. And I'm okay with it!

When it comes to my social media presence, with the exception of my Facebook and Snapchat accounts, everything is public. I really don't pay much mind to my following because I'm more concerned about the quality of content. An "if you build it, they will come" mentality. When asked if I wish I had more followers, my answer is always no. I like to be able to engage with my followers and the more you have, the more overwhelming it is to keep up. The truth is, my first Instagram account topped out at over 50,000 followers before I shut it down. The stress of having that many eyes on me and that many people trying to get a piece of me was overwhelming. It came with a lot of admiration, but there was also a lot of hate coming my way. I didn't like the idea of that many people having access to me so I deleted the account.

Does that mean it's gone? Of course not! Instagram (owned by Facebook who does the same when you want to leave) merely deactivated the account and made it invisible. Should I want to return to it, I just need to log in again and BOOM, there it is. I won't be doing that mostly because I only have a vague idea what the password for that account is, and I'm not going back to that nonsense.

In the long run, my advice is always and forever going to be the same. Think of your friends list like a game of golf: the lower the score, the better. Treat your friends and followers lists like a VIP Red Carpet experience: only the best names possible make the cut. Keep your accounts private and locked up tight. When you get a friend or follow request, take the time to really consider it before hitting that "accept" button. As a rule for myself, I do not accept requests from someone I have never been in the same room with. Additionally, I won't accept requests from people who are not already a contact in my phone. Even if we have mutual friends in common, if I don't know who you are, you're not on the list.

If you're not 100% certain of the identity of someone, you shouldn't be giving them full access to your accounts and posts. It has become far too easy for people to pretend to be someone they are not and I'm not just talking about faking a glamorous life for Instagram. As a matter of fact, the Better Business Bureau has reported a marked increase in catfishing and romance scams.[46] While many platforms are working to make it more difficult to create fake accounts, it's still too easy and sadly there are some pretty awful people out there in the world.

The homework assignment I give every audience, regardless of age, is to take a good look at those friends and followers lists. I'm going to ask you to do the same. This is actually something I do about once a month. I'll sit down with my Facebook and Instagram and remove people. It's nothing personal, but more a matter of safety. As of this writing, I have 422 friends on Facebook, and I know every last one of them. They are family, friends, co-workers and classmates. I will not hesitate to remove any one of them. If we don't talk that often or I know they don't use their account that much, I kick them off the list. You are able to do this on Instagram as well. Click on your followers and when the list comes up, you'll see that you have the option to remove yourself from their follow list.

This is also a great time to take a look at the accounts you are following. This is something I did during the great pandemic lockdown of 2020 when I went from following over 1000 accounts down to around 500. I pulled out some Marie Kondo moves and asked myself whether or not these accounts were sparking joy. Seriously. I took a long hard look and asked, "Does following this person make me happy or make me miserable?" Turns out many of those people were not sparking joy in my life and making me feel bad that I wasn't making sourdough bread.

I also disabled notifications for my accounts which did wonderful things for my mental health. I wasn't so inclined to look at my phone every few minutes to check for new likes and follows. Sure, I see them when I log in, but they are not driving my life and it helps keep me off my phone so much when I should be worrying about other things. I can't recommend this move enough and, believe it or not, science agrees with me.

Social media apps are designed to get our attention; the more time we spend on them, the more money they get from their advertisers. Additionally, when we see those likes and follows, it actually causes our brains to release dopamine, a neurotransmitter that makes us feel good.[47] Our brains are big fans of the happy chemicals, and we are wired to get quick fixes of them whenever we can. So a quick check of Instagram or Twitter can turn into five, ten, thirty minutes of mindless scrolling. Sure, I joke about falling down the YouTube rabbit holes, but it's a very real time-suck.

All of this is to say, please make sure you are being safe out there. Keep an eye on who has access to your information in the form of being your friend or follower. Sure, we'd all love to see something we create go viral, but make sure you're doing all of that for the right reasons. I think of my blog posts that have gone viral over the years and I'm actually quite proud that, even though I'm not famous as a result, each of them had an important message to deliver. Going viral wasn't my end goal in writing them; sure, the more of an audience the merrier, but delivering an important message was more vital to me. Let that be important to you.

screen-free time

I will be the first to admit that the amount of time I spend in front of screens is not only embarrassing, but makes me sick to think about. I'm talking about my phone, the computer, my Nintendo Switch, my tablet, and my laptop. According to a report from eMarketer, screen time in the United States has jumped significantly in the past couple years and is poised to surpass eight hours a day by 2022.[48] Sure, when looking at 2020 we can blame the COVID-19 pandemic, but part of me fears that the number will grow rather than shrink as time goes on.

My job is in social media so my screen time is beyond insane when I take the time to think about it, worse when I'm writing a book because of how much time I spend on the computer either writing or researching. Then the time I spend on my own personal social media as well as the professional accounts that I manage. Then the 45 minutes or so I spend on my Animal Crossing island (don't judge me) plus reading ebooks and catching up on the latest episode of Ted Lasso. By the time I've set my head down on my bed, I've logged more hours on digital devices than I'd care to admit. For the sake of transparency, I'm personally logging about 12 hours a day on some sort of device while I'm working on this book which is about 4 hours above average.

As of a 2019 Common Sense Media report, teens ages 13-18 were spending about 7 hours and 22 minutes in front of a screen.[49] Here's what their breakdown looks like:

- TV/Videos 2 Hours 52 Minutes
- Gaming 1 Hour 36 Minutes
- Social Media 1 Hour 10 Minutes
- Internet Surfing 37 Minutes
- Video-Chatting 19 Minutes
- E-Reading 8 Minutes

- Content Creation 12 Minutes
- Other 28 Minutes

As of this writing, that report is over 2 years old. Think about how much those numbers have possibly changed in that time. Take some time to think about your own screen usage, how do you break down? Here's a homework assignment for you! Spend one week logging the amount of time you spend on your devices. It adds up pretty quick and the answer may surprise you!

How do you compare to that average of 7 hours and 22 minutes? More? Less? Either way, I recommend working to try and reduce that time as much as possible. I can promise the moment I'm done writing this book, I plan on taking a serious screen break! I've also taken the time to make minor adjustments here and there to help reduce my own time.

One of the first things I did was move my cell phone out of my bedroom. This alone prevented me from jumping onto it the moment I woke up in the morning and eliminated the temptation to mindlessly scroll Instagram before bed. Additionally, I no longer read on my tablet before bed and instead pick up a good, old-fashioned book to consume for a bit. The jury still seems to be out about whether or not ereaders are detrimental to sleep cycles, but considering my tablet lets me access all my social apps, I'd rather not have the temptation.

As I mentioned in the previous chapter, I've also turned off notifications from social media apps and instead see them when I log in. This keeps my phone from pinging or buzzing at all hours and reduces the temptation of just "popping on to check," only to lose 20 minutes mindlessly scrolling. It has also done wonders for my mental health in that I'm not constantly worrying about the validation of receiving "likes" on something once I've posted. I post and move on with my life. Even better is when I can schedule posts ahead of time and forget about them completely until I log in.

This is a great way to not only remind yourself what is truly important, but also helps you be more present for others. You're not in a deep conversation or any conversation and constantly being distracted by your phone going off. It's important to remember that our phones are a tool, not something that should be controlling every minute of our lives. Not every comment, text or email needs an immediate response, especially during your personal time. You get to decide when you want to engage and you're not living in reactive mode 24/7 which is unhealthy and draining.

It feels counterintuitive suggesting you watch something to highlight my points but *Black Mirror* is often a great commentary on our obsession with technology and social media, specifically the episode "Nosedive" in which a young woman's obsession with her social media status ultimately leads to her downfall. Honestly, I wanted to throw away my phone after watching it. "Smithereens" is also an interesting addition to the series and touches on the addictive nature of social media. Katy Perry's music video for "Chained to the Rhythm" was also an amazing commentary on our obsession with "likes", "followers" and social media as a whole along with the astounding fakeness of it all.

I'm not saying that we should throw every piece of technology out the window and go back to the Stone Age. No one wants that. I still shudder thinking about having to hand write reports back in elementary school. I'm a lefty, handwriting isn't fun for us, especially when my teachers required it to be done in a blue pen which is my mortal enemy. Instead I'm recommending finding ways to move away from screen time whenever possible.

One of the ways I do this is with a piece of wearable technology, my FitBit. I use it as a reminder to step away from the computer screen and walk around a bit, either around my apartment or I'll take myself outside and get some of that sweet Vitamin D. Until I am reminded that I live in Florida and the sun is just angry all of the time or the clouds are angry and a monsoon hits. The point is to make sure we aren't just turning into those people from *Wall-E* and that we are getting away from our tech and move around.

I also make sure to set limits for myself each day. I have a shut down time and no matter what, I stick to it. If it happens while I'm writing and I want to keep going, I'll move to the old fashioned notebook and pen to get the rest of my thoughts out if there is a need. I'll also do this with my TV watching and limit myself to a set amount of time or number of episodes. I'm actually happy that some streaming services are releasing episodes weekly (old school style) rather than season dumps so I am less tempted to sit and binge watch.

I'll sometimes engage in a digital detox and swear off everything for a period of time. I'll pick a day or even a whole weekend where I will shut it all down and allow myself time to really enjoy life in the real world. This is actually a big reason why I love going on cruises because nothing works unless you pay an obscene amount of money for the Internet plan and I'm too cheap for that, so I'm able to be screen free for the duration of the trip. The world can wait to see all my fun photos; I'm too focused on trivia nights and karaoke.

I also encourage my friends to do the same for themselves, even if just in small doses. One of my biggest pet peeves is when a friend asks to hang out and then spends the entire time on their phone. I'll admit, I can be guilty of this as well; but if I haven't seen you in a while, I'm going to focus on you instead of my phone. One of my favorite things in the world is Cell Phone Jenga when out with friends. Everyone places their phone in a pile on the table and the first person to pick it up during the meal has to pay the tab. Take some time off your phone and appreciate what's right in front of you.

If you don't want to listen to me, that's fine, but you should listen to Beyonce. One of my favorite stories occurred in 2013 at a Beyonce concert when Queen B was performing in Atlanta. She was interacting with the crowd when one fan was too focused on recording what was happening rather than experiencing it, shouting out "I'm in your face, baby. You gotta seize the moment!"[50]

We need to stop living life through the looking glass and realize that the real world is right in front of us. I understand wanting to snap a few pictures to remember this moment, but let it just be that moment. Sit back and enjoy the ride while it lasts. I am just as guilty sometimes so don't think I'm trying to preach to you, I'm writing all this down as much for me as for you. Let's work together to reduce our time behind the screen and increase our time in the real world!

life in the times of fake news

Are y'all ready for a sentence that is going to make me sound super old? Like, I wrote it and then I needed to step away for a minute and really take the time to think about my life. Actually, the whole paragraph will make me sound like an old fart to the teens and your parents are going to chuckle to themselves and say "Yep". Okay, now I'm back to being excited about it so let's do it!

Back in my day, when we were writing any sort of research paper we had to use the encyclopedia to do it.

The encyclopedia, books, magazines and maybe some videos if we were lucky. Those papers were written by hand in the aforementioned blue ink and had to be cited in MLA format. I laugh every time I do a citation for this book because I'm very likely not following any real format and just doing my own thing and teachers everywhere are cringing. But I digress.

When the Internet came along and became more prevalent in homes and educational settings, we were still cautioned against using it for information unless the information came from a reputable and recognizable source like CNN or *National Geographic*. This was a time when Wikipedia was in its infancy and using it as a source would lead you to an automatic failure. Y'all, I'm telling you the late 90's and early 2000's were a crazy time. Britney Spears used to do mall tours. Like, a concert, in a mall. Madness.

In recent years the term "fake news" has permeated our vernacular and is now a favorite term amongst politicians and news pundits. With the Internet having become a mass and open collective that anyone in the world can contribute to, it has become harder and harder to determine what is real and what is fake. It's also not helpful when those same politicians and news pundits are sprouting their own lies into the world, but that is a topic for another book.

What's important is being able to discern what is real and what is fake when it comes to the world around you, whether you are researching a paper for school, a book about teens and social media, or just learning about the world in general. I use this book as an example because it is the reality that I am currently living in. As I want to talk about a certain topic or particular incident in the news, I turn to Google to help me out just like you would. The key is not clicking on the first result that pops up and taking it as fact. Digging a little deeper is important because one story might not have all the information you need or, may be older and outdated. At any given point in time, I probably have 10-20 tabs open while I'm writing and I'm bouncing all over to make sure I have the best, correct information.

When it comes to research and the news, there is a lot out there and, sadly, much of it can't be trusted. We have seen a lot of this when it came to COVID-19 and the vaccines and all the disinformation that flooded the Internet and social media through all of 2020 and leading into the elections that year. It was a frustrating and scary time. Headlines are written to be "clickbait" or content designed to attract attention and encourage visitors to click on their page. Sensational headlines get attention and get shared, leading to advertising money for the website. Often people will share these articles without actually reading them and end up aiding in the spread of misinformation which, in cases like the coronavirus, threaten people's safety.

Many social media companies have been working hard to crack down on the spread of misinformation and have been targeting keywords and dispatching their own fact checkers. In January, 2021 Twitter launched a program called Birdwatch which was designed to help fight misinformation on their platform. Others, like Facebook and Instagram, have gone after keywords and any post using them will come with a disclaimer. Currently, anything mentioning COVID-19 regardless of what the post is, will automatically include a link to the CDC's website, offering up the best, most factual information.

Project Look Sharp recommends asking yourself these questions when you encounter information on the web, especially if it seems sensationalized:

- Who made this?
- Who is the target audience?
- Who paid for this?
- Who gets paid if you click on this?
- Who might benefit or be harmed by this message?
- What is left out of this message that might be important?
- Is this credible (and what makes you think that?)

After you've asked yourself those questions, remember not to take everything you see and read at face value. Do a little investigating of your own before sharing a link or taking what you've read as fact. I've fallen victim to this myself, so just know that it happens to the best of us, and it's nothing to be ashamed of; it's all a part of growing up and learning. Keep an eye out for unusual URLs or even website names that have been designed to trick a reader into believing they are legitimate. As you read the articles, pay attention to the style and quality of what you're reading. Look for sources and other clues that you should be skeptical about what you are seeing.

Clickbait is also designed to elicit an emotional response and get an extreme reaction from the reader. Check in on your emotions because it could be a sign that you are being messed with or the outlet is really vying for your click. For example, as I just took a moment to check my own social media, an article caught my attention on Facebook. It shows a photo of the six main actors from the show *Friends* with a headline reading "'*Friends* Star Announces Battle With Cancer." Though I was never the biggest fan of the show, the headline caught my attention and I clicked on it. It was revealed that the actor, James Michael Tyler, who played a supporting character on the show has cancer.

The heartbreaking story is true, but look at the methods used to get me to click the link: a photo of the primary cast along with a vague headline.

Another big question to ask when presented with potential misinformation is: are mainstream news outlets also reporting what you are reading? While not a definitive answer to the authenticity of the piece, it could be a step in the right direction of letting you know what is real and what isn't. When in doubt, search Google or Wikipedia for some clues as to what is really going on (just writing that is a sign as to how much has changed in the 20 years since Wikipedia launched).[51]

share kindness

It's October 1, 2010 and 11-year-old Shawn Walsh is dressed in a yellow plaid shirt standing at the altar of the First Baptist Church in Tehachapi, California. Before him is a standing-room-only crowd of hundreds. So many people showed up to the church on this day that they couldn't be contained within its walls. The pews are filled to bursting and people have taken seats wherever they can, including cramming into the middle aisle of the church. On the white walls behind him, a photo montage plays of his older brother

Seth. A picture of Seth wearing a tiara and a big smile appears, the next frame just features a single word with a slash through it: *bullying.*

Gripping the microphone Shawn talks about how his older brother could be "a pain in the butt" at times, but that Seth was "the best big brother in the world- no, the galaxy." The montage continues behind him as Shawn references the cause of his brother's death. "I always wanted to protect him," he says. "I just wish people could have been nice to him like my mom taught me."

On September 19, 2010 Seth's mother, Wendy, had found him unconscious; he had tried to hang himself from a tree in his backyard after an apparent bullying incident that took place in a park near his house. The incident was just one of many Seth had endured for years, having been harassed in school and online for his sexual orientation. Seth was rushed to a hospital after his mother found him. He died on September 27th.[52]

When people ask me why I got into speaking about bullying prevention and online safety, I tell them about Seth. I tell them about Tyler Clementi, Tyler Long, Jamey Rodemeyer, Megan Meir, and Phoebe Prince. I tell them about the countless young people whose lives were robbed from them because of hate. I tell them how bullying affected me when I was their age and how easily their stories could have been mine.

The concept of bullying isn't anything new; it has been around since the dawn of time. In the time before the Internet, bullying existed in three forms: physical, verbal, and relational. The popularity of social networking sites and messaging apps led to the evolution of bullying as it took on a digital form as cyberbullying.

Cyberbullying changed the game because of the ease of access bullies had to their victims. Traditional bullying takes place in the face-to-face world whereas cyberbullying can be accomplished anywhere. The Internet gave us all round-the-clock access to one another and bullying is now played out for the entire world to see. Some apps give the bully the ability to be anonymous or create a fake identity with which to attack their victim and all of it is permanent and difficult to escape.

I have spent well over a decade travelling to schools all over North America. I have spoken to well over one million students, parents, and educators on this very topic and there's something powerful I've learned over this time. When it comes to bullying, I can talk about it all day long to an audience. I can share stories like Seth's, or Phoebe's or Megan's. Educators, politicians and even celebrities can talk themselves raw on the topic, but at the end of the day that's really all any of us can do: talk.

It is the action that *you* decide to take that makes the real difference. At the end of the day, this is your world. Your teachers and administrators, those politicians and celebrities, and even me can do all we can to give you the right tools and point you in the right direction, but it's up to you to make the difference. To hear those stories and say "Not here, not in my community. Those stories will not become ours."

When it comes to bullying most people typically just think of the bully and the victim, but the reality is there is almost always a third person involved: the bystander. This is someone who witnesses the bullying take place and either help the bully, help the victim, or do nothing at all. These bystanders are classified as hurtful, helpful and passive. I feel it's important to recognize the role the bystander plays in bullying because they are the ones with the power to do the most good in a bullying situation.

Often, victims don't report the bullying; one report showing that upwards of 64% of victims of bullying don't report the incident(s).[53] Many fear further retaliation, making the bullying worse. If the bullying is online, they might be afraid of losing digital access if they tell their parents about what's happening. In many cases, victims may feel ashamed or embarrassed about the situation and not want to speak up about it or might not even know how to go about reporting the bullying.

Following a rash of bullying-related suicides in 2009 and 2010, many states went to work creating or strengthening their anti-bullying laws. In 2012 California passed "Seth's Law" which was designed to strengthen existing anti-bullying laws in the state. Like many of the other laws talked about in this book, anti-bullying laws are dealt with on a state level. There are no federal laws directly targeting bullying, but there are times when bullying behavior overlaps with discriminatory harassment. When these overlaps happen, federally-funded schools are required to resolve the harassment.

Many schools have worked on their own to enhance their bullying prevention efforts including updating policies, creating ways for students to report bullying and even bringing in educational programs to help educate their staff, students, and communities. Again, all of these are great steps, but it's up to those same educators, students, and community members to take action. Think about how you felt reading about Seth's story, reading about his brother speaking at his funeral, his mother finding him unconscious. Take that feeling and turn it into action.

Does your school have anti-bullying policies? When was the last time they were updated? Do they include cyberbullying? Does your school have a reporting procedure? Do you know what it is? Does your school have a bullying prevention specialist on staff? Do you know who they are? Am I asking too many questions?

The point of my line of questioning is to inspire you to be proactive rather than reactive. Many states passed new or improved anti-bullying laws after a tragedy occured. Had these laws been in place sooner, things might have been very different for a lot of the victims of bullying. When you look at stories like Seth Walsh's you'll see these incidents of bullying were reported time and time again, and those in charge chose to do nothing about it. Now the law requires them to. This is another reason why so much bullying goes unreported, because kids feel that nothing is going to be done about it.

If you don't know the answers to those questions, take some time and learn for yourself. A good chunk of schools have their handbook and policies on their websites so go check them out. This is something I do with every school I visit. I take a long hard look at their policies and will offer recommendations on what could be improved if anything. Depending on what state you live in, take your policy and compare it to schools in

New Jersey or Massachusetts where they have some of the strictest anti-bullying laws in the country. Unfortunately, these laws were reactionary following bullying-related suicides within their borders. If you feel like your school doesn't measure up, then do something about it. Meet with your school counselor or administrators and work with them to improve the policies.

When it comes to my advice for victims of bullying, I like to share the advice that was given to me when I was in high school. I've added a bit to it when it comes to the cyberbullying front, but I've found these are the best things to do when it comes to bullying:

DON'T RESPOND

Bullies are all about power and they gain satisfaction in knowing that they have control over someone. When their victim doesn't respond or acknowledge them, they lose some of that power. Sometimes the best way to respond is to just walk away from the situation if at all possible. The same goes for online bullying. More often than not, when people don't engage with the behavior it will resolve itself. This may not always be the case, but this is a good first step in dealing with a bully.

DON'T RETALIATE

This is a hard one and I am very understanding of that fact. When someone attacks us, hurts us, we want to fight back. Our every instinct can be to fight back, but this only puts the victim in a position to be labeled a bully as well and get themselves in trouble. Obviously, if someone is in physical danger and backed into a corner, by all means, defend yourself. But in many cases, particularly cyberbullying, an eye for an eye is never the ideal response.

SAVE THE EVIDENCE

When it comes to cyberbullying in particular, the upside is the evidence is right there. Screenshoot conversations, save text messages, and keep a log of what is happening. This way you have what you need to prove there is a situation of bullying going on. If the bullying is happening in the real world, record what happened to the best of your ability in a notebook or as a note on your phone. Who was involved and who was there to witness what happened?

BLOCK THE BULLY

One of the many upsides of social media is that if you don't want someone talking to you, you can block them. This is a common feature among many popular social networks and applications and I highly encourage everyone to take advantage of them. There are even features on your phone that can be used to block texts and calls from certain numbers. It's honestly the feature I love the most and I use it often.

TALK TO A TRUSTED ADULT

It's easy to feel like you're alone, especially when you are being hurt, harassed and picked on by others. What I can promise you is that you are never alone and there will always be someone out there who cares about your safety and well-being. Whether it is a teacher, administrator, parent or relative, it's important to share with someone what is going on. They can help work through the situation and offer resources. In many states, it is the law that schools investigate any and all claims of bullying and harassment so let the system work for you. This is why I encourage you to look at your school's policies and help create a system for reporting that allows for anonymous reports or multiple options for who to talk to.

BE A FRIEND, NOT A BYSTANDER

It's important to realize that when you witness situations of bullying, whether online or off, and you do nothing, say nothing, you are just as guilty as the bully; you are just as responsible for what happens to the victim. It's important to be an upstander in these situations and give voice to them. This can be as simple as involving an adult when you see something happening. The important thing is to do something to help the situation rather than ignoring it completely. Obviously, don't put yourself in a dangerous situation where you may be physically harmed, but do run and grab a teacher or other adult or call the police depending on the situation.

TAKE TIME TO THINK

If there is one message I hope has been drilled into your head the most in this book, above all, the biggest thing I will ask of you is to take the time to think: to think about yourself and your classmates on a human level. To know that, regardless of what we think we know about each other, we are all human beings with thoughts, emotions and dreams. It's important to re-member that as we go about our day-to-day lives; we are all fighting different battles. I want you to think about Seth Walsh. I want you to think about his broth-er Shawn. I want you to think of the countless brothers, sisters, mothers, fathers, friends, families, communities that have all lost someone.

Know that your words and actions hold a lot of power and it's up to you whether you plan on using that power for good or evil. I completely understand how wildly dramatic that sounds but it is the honest truth. English author Edward Bulwer-Lytton said it best in his play *Richelieu; Or the Conspiracy*: "the pen is mightier than the sword." Words have the power to give life, but they also have the power to take it away. Use them wisely.

CYBERBULLIES

When it comes to bullies in the online world, it's important that you take steps to protect yourself. Taking a look at privacy settings and friends lists are key to ensuring that bullies are kept out. Everyone wants the highest friend and follower count possible these days, but that "Internet fame" comes with a heavy price. It's important to keep things like phone numbers and screen names private. The same goes for passwords. Teens are, all too often, far too comfortable sharing passwords with friends and this is a practice that needs to be ended. I always recommend treating your password like your toothbrush: don't share it with anyone and change it often. End the practice of putting phone numbers or usernames for messaging apps into your public bios. The less access you give to potential bullies, the easier life will be.

When it comes to the digital world, it's very easy to forget that the real world exists and when you are posting hurtful things, there's a very real human being on the receiving end of those words. It's easy to think that it all goes away when you power down for the night, but those words, those memes, those screenshots are all still out there floating around the cyber universe. It's hard to forget the permanence of it all.

I think about a school I visited in Washington state a number of years ago. I was brought in to speak to the students and parents following a serious cyberbullying incident where a 6th grade girl was being harassed by a group of students. They would tease her in the hallways and created a Facebook group dedicated to making fun of her. The group grew in size and included people that didn't even go to school with these bullies or the young woman.

She ultimately found the page and would watch as, day after day, her classmates would make fun of her hair, her clothes, and her weight. One afternoon, following a gym class, one of the girls involved in the Facebook group, snapped a picture of her victim as she was changing and posted it to the group with an obscene caption and soon other comments began rolling in:

She's so ugly!
She's so fat!
She should kill herself.

The photo was made into a series of vicious memes that soon found their way out of the Facebook group and onto other platforms like Instagram and Twitter. There was no escaping it as it made its way around the world. All of this playing out on this young woman's phone with no chance of stopping it.

As a result of the teasing and mean comments, she started making herself sick. She would refuse meals or would make herself throw up after eating in a dangerous attempt to lose weight. It wasn't until after she passed out in a physical education class and ended up in the hospital that the bullying came to light. The creators and participants in the Facebook page were punished by detentions and suspensions and the page was reported to and removed by Facebook.

But, thinking about what we've talked about so far in these pages, what does that really mean? Are those images gone? Are those comments gone? Those memes?

No.

Sure, maybe by now they have been buried by the enormity of the Internet, replaced by whatever the latest memes are. But once it's out there, it's out there forever. And for that young woman, they live forever in her memories. Thankfully, she got the help she needed and overcame the hurt and harassment, but those words will live with her forever.

It's one thing to say mean and hurtful things to a person's face. You have to see their reaction, their pain. Perhaps that will stir up some empathy in you, make you regret those words and actions. It's another thing to type them out on a screen and send them out into the world where you don't have to be face-to-face with your target.

These are the stories I want you to keep in mind as you navigate your way around the online world. I want them to live forever in your mind as they do in mine. I want them to be that little voice in your head, reminding you to spread kindness rather than hate. I want that voice to remind you to stand up for others who might not be able to stand up for themselves. I want you to go out there and be the good in the world.

pay attention to the real world

In 2011 three teens in Utah lost their lives attempting to get themselves the perfect selfie. "Standing right by a train ahaha this is awesome!" was the caption posted by Savannah Webster along with a selfie featuring her, her older sister Kelsea and their friend Essa. The three posed for the selfie while standing on train tracks as a train passed by them on a nearby set of tracks, the wind whipping their hair for the photo. What they didn't notice in the background of the disturbing photo before posting it, was the headlight of the oncoming train in the distance behind them on the very track on which they were standing.

"They were in their own little world," recalled the train's conductor John Anderson who frantically blasted the train's horn to get the attention of the girls. The noise from the train passing them on the opposite track blocked Anderson's attempt to get their attention.

Unlike a car, a train can't swerve out of the way of an obstacle, and can take up to a mile before they come to a complete stop when travelling 55 miles per hour. The train struck the girls going 39 miles an hour, killing Kelsea and Essa instantly. The train didn't come to a complete stop until about a quarter of a mile down the tracks. John found Savannah clinging to life and sat, comforting the teen while waiting for the paramedics to arrive. The 13-year-old had more than a dozen broken bones, internal bleeding, blood clots, and severe brain injury. She died three days after the accident.[54]

Stories like this are, sadly, not uncommon, but often get lost in the noise and misleading nature of the digital world. As I was writing out the above story I was also texting with a friend of mine. I realized that I was being a bit of a downer in our conversation and apologized, explaining that I was working and reading the articles and transcripts around this story was really bringing me down.

His response was, "Wait, that's actually a true story?!"

"Yeah," I told him, "it's one of way too many similar stories."

In 2015 Anna User and a friend, two Romanian teenagers, went hunting to take the perfect selfie and found themselves at a train station in the town of Iași. Ignoring the warnings of a passer-by, the two climbed on top of a stationary train to snap selfies. Anna was laying on top of the train and stuck her foot in the air as she snapped her perfect selfie. An electrical field surrounding the cables above the train sent 27,000 volts rushing through her body, causing her to burst into flames. The jolt sent her friend flying from the train. The two were rushed to the hospital and while Anna's friend eventually recovered from her injuries, Ursa died as a result of the accident.[55]

I've said it before and I'll say it again, we live in a very fast-paced world, but it's important to slow ourselves down. Don't let your entire life revolve around social media and technology. Like I said before, all of these apps and devices are tools, not a way of life. We don't need to capture everything and we sure don't need to be taking wild risks for the sake of an Instagram post or a TikTok video.

This is another big reason why I'm a major proponent of turning off notifications from social media apps to help eliminate the distraction, not just from getting work done but from your day-to-day life. At this point it probably wouldn't be too outside the realm of possibility to say that everyone knows at least one person who was in a texting-related accident in a car.

In August of 2010 a 19-year-old Missouri man was driving his pick-up truck for his normal morning commute when he rammed into the back of a tractor trailer, causing a chain reaction of accidents. A school bus behind him on the highway crashed into him and a second bus crashed into the first. The resulting pile-up took the life of the pick-up's driver along with a 15-year-old student on one of the busses, 38 others were seriously injured.[56]

Federal investigators from the National Transportation Safety Board discovered that the driver of the pickup had been texting at the time of the accident. A total of 11 texts had been sent and received in the moments leading up to the crash, the final text occurring just before his truck crashed into the semi in front of him, causing the pile-up.[57] While it is impossible to know whether he was actively typing, reaching for the phone, or reading a text at the time of the accident, it is clear that his focus was not 100% on the task of safely driving.

The National Safety Council reports that cell phone use while driving leads to roughly 1.6 million car accidents a year which accounts for about 64% of auto accidents in the US. In the same report they mention that many causes of automobile accidents aren't reported properly so there's a very good chance that number is significantly higher.[58] These accidents have resulted in over 400,000 injuries and 3,142 deaths.[5960] Teen drivers are four times more likely to get into an accident while using their cell phone and an average of 11 teens die every day in texting-related car accidents.[61]

No text or selfie or TikTok video is worth your or anyone else's life. I know what it's like to feel young and untouchable, what it feels like to be infinite. I'll admit I'm guilty of some pretty unsafe behavior and was fortunate enough not to get hurt. I've also had some really stupid close calls that could have gotten me or someone else seriously injured. I'm not willing to wait for a wake-up call on this and you shouldn't be either. Take steps to keep yourself safe out there in the real world just as I want you to take them towards being safe in the online world.

JOSH GUNDERSON

check in on your real world health

Social media truly is a wonderful tool. As someone who spends a great deal of time travelling, it's nice to be able to check in with family and friends and share some of my adventures. Friends will offer up great local places to check out for dinner or sight-seeing and I will share pictures and funny thoughts from the road. As my siblings are pretty spread out all over the place, it's a nice tool for us to share quick updates. It was also a great way to stay connected with the world when we all found ourselves locked down in our homes at the beginning of the COVID-19 pandemic.

I promised early on that I wasn't going to bash on social media and this is why! I'm a daily user of multiple platforms and I have no place to tell others not to use it because that would just make me a hypocrite. But, I do recognize the toll social media can take on my mental health. I will say because of social media's relative newness to the world, there are currently no long-term studies on its effects on mental health, but there has been some research that indicates that social networking does have an impact.

Why is that?

The answer is simple: dopamine!

I will be honest that every scholarly article I found explaining the brain chemical to me was super boring and I have no way of getting Bill Nye the Science Guy or Miss Frizzle here to explain it, so I'll just break it down like this: Dopamine is a chemical produced by our brains that plays a starring role in motivating our behavior. When does the brain release this wonderful chemical? It happens when we bite into a particularly delicious piece of food, after exercise, and even after we've had successful social interactions. Basically it's our brain's way of giving us a gold star for behaviors that are beneficial and motivates us to repeat that action. So it's my brain's fault I ate an entire sleeve of cookies while working on this chapter.

I have zero idea why the medical journals I read couldn't just explain it like that in the first place but here we are. I was actually super tempted to explain it using a quote from *Legally Blonde* but it turns out she was talking about endorphins and according to the Internet those are kind of but not really the same as dopamine so it wouldn't have worked. It's probably too late to get them to change the script.

You are probably wondering what this has to do with social media. According to a study conducted by Harvard University it was found that when a person received the notification of a "like," comment, or mention, the brain receives a rush of dopamine and sends it along the reward pathways of the brain, causing the person to feel pleasure.[62] Now social media has provided a seemingly endless source of immediate rewards in the form of attention from others. The brain then begins to rewire itself through this positive reinforcement, making users desire likes, shares, comments, and followers. Soon, it becomes an addiction. Seriously! Those same studies showed that those positive reactions on social media light up the same parts of the brain as gambling or recreational drug use.

Some studies about social media and mental health have also revealed there's a correlation between social media use and depression. A landmark study published in the *Journal of Social and Clinical Psychology* in 2018 found that limiting social media use actually shows a decrease in loneliness and depression.[63]

In an effort to establish the link between social media and depression, the researchers assigned 143 students from the University of Pennsylvania to two different groups. One group could use social media with no restrictions, while the second group had their access to social media limited to just 30 minutes on Facebook, Instagram, and Snapchat a week over a three-week period. To ensure compliance in the study, iPhones were used and the researchers monitored the data.

The group of students whose access to social media was restricted reported a lower severity of depression and loneliness than they had at the beginning of the study. Surprisingly, both groups reported a drop in anxiety and FOMO (fear of missing out) because the simple act of participating in the study even made the group with unrestricted access realize just how much time they were dedicating to social media each day.[64]

I share this because it's important to realize that all of this connection to the entire world can really take its toll on our mental health. We saw a lot of this during the coronavirus lockdowns when some people were handling things just fine and baking, and making art, and participating in workout challenges. Some people weren't having such a great time and seeing others thrive while they were silently suffering didn't help much.

Social media has the power to give users a strong case of FOMO. Take, for instance, a classmate throwing a party and posting about it. You were invited, but weren't able to attend for whatever reason. Worse, a classmate is throwing a party and posting about it and you weren't invited at all. You may find yourself feeling hurt, sad and lonely seeing that you were left out while, perhaps, others in your social circle were invited.

Doomscrolling, or absorption of constant bad news, also can take a severe toll on one's mental health. I saw this a lot in 2020 amongst my friends who work in social media marketing. A big part of their job is being on top of what is trending in the news and social media. This means frequent exposure to some not-so-great things like natural disasters, terrorist attacks, political strife, and celebrity deaths. Even I found myself miserable every time I had to scroll through my Twitter feed being bombarded with COVID deaths, police brutality, and the constant onslaught of everything about the 2020 presidential elections.

If you are someone whospends a significant amount of time on social media, make sure you do some self check-ins on your own mental health. If you're feeling sad, depressed, frustrated, and lonely, it may be time to re-evaluate your online habits and take some time away from the screen. Switch over to things that bring a smile to your face. My recommendations include playing with a cat, taking a walk outside, or going to a local animal shelter and requesting to cuddle with any and all puppies who need just as much love as you. Then, when no one is looking, steal all the puppies and you'll all live happily ever after.

For legal reasons I should point out that that last sentence was a joke. Please do not commit puppy-related robbery. Not a good look for any of us. However, that headline would give people a reason to smile while doomscrolling: "Reader Steals Adorable Puppies at the Behest of A Guy Who Told Them to Spend Less Time Online." It's very click-baity, but I'm sure they'll all appreciate the break from real bad news and chuckle about something. What I'm saying is: follow your heart, but make sure nothing is traced back to me.

The moral of the story is, make sure you are finding a balance in your life when it comes to the amount of time you are spending on social media and the Internet as a whole. When it comes to who/what you are following, make sure they are creators and people who inspire you rather than make you feel horrible. One of my favorite authors, Jonathan Maberry, is a lot of fun to follow all across social media because he posts wonderful memes, talks about what he has going on, and encourages his followers to share their victories with him or tell him something he doesn't know. Follow those who are going to make you happy and pay attention to those who don't and get them out of there. Marie Kondo would be proud.

so what now?

We've made it to the end of the book! Were this one of my in-person programs I would take this time to recap what we just learned and open the floor to questions. It feels a bit odd to do the first part (it's not going to stop me) and the second bit would be impossible. Maybe that's the next big idea! When you buy an ebook, there's a link you can click to go to a Q&A with the author. I guess if you *do* have questions you can feel free to email me. Just go to the "contact" page on my website and feel free to pick my mind. I do my best to read and respond to messages as soon as possible depending on how busy I am at the time and whether I'm on the road.

I will point out my favorite time in a workshop is right about the end when I put my contact information on the screen and there's inevitably one student that chastises me for giving out my information right after I got through telling them not to give out theirs. I assure you, the information you find on my website is all business and my personal email is just that. The reason I do share my email is because I want you to know that you have one more adult on your side, should you have questions.

The biggest thing I want to remind you of while I still have you, is the big point I have been pushing this entire time: take time to think! When you are posting online, when you are sharing information, when you are interacting with others, when you find yourself spending too much time on your devices, when you find yourself tempted to check a text while you're driving: stop and think first. Additionally, it's always okay to slow down and disconnect when it all feels a bit too much.

For me, one of the best things that came out of the COVID pandemic lockdowns was that I was forced to slow down. I was constantly moving at a million miles an hour and missing so much. I kept myself busy to the point of exhaustion and I was stressed beyond belief. I was constantly overbooking myself and saying yes to everyone and everything. A lot changed when I had no choice but to pump the brakes and it wasn't easy. I was depressed, anxious and never felt more alone in my life.

You didn't see that on social media, did you? Of course not! Why would I put anything other than the bright and shiny on there? You saw jokes and smiling faces and memes from me. I tweeted about social distancing and all the other buzzwords we were using. (Is anyone else sick of "new normal"?) I blogged about Animal Crossing and how much fun I was having making my little haunted island.

What you see on social media isn't always real life. A prime example that came to light recently was the struggle of Britney Spears who has famously been under a conservatorship for the past 13 years. Despite an explosive documentary and the #FreeBritney movement, she was constantly posting videos and images on her Instagram telling the world that she was happy and doing just fine. That all changed when she came forward with the harsh truth in June, 2021.

"I've lied and told the whole world, 'I'm OK, I'm happy,' " she said. "I've been in denial, I've been in shock. I am traumatized."[65]

She took to her own Instagram saying:

"I just want to tell you guys a little secret... I believe as people we all want the fairy tale life and by the way I've posted... my life seems to look and be pretty amazing... I think that's what we all strive for!!!! That was one of my mother's best traits... no matter how sh*tty a day was when I was younger... for the sake of me and my siblings she always pretended like everything was ok. I'm bringing this to people's attention because I don't want people to think my life is perfect because IT'S DEFINITELY NOT AT ALL... and if you have read anything about me in the news this week... you obviously really know now it's not!!!! I apologize for pretending like I've been ok the past two years... I did it because of my pride and I was embarrassed to share what happened to me... but honestly who doesn't want to capture their Instagram in a fun light?"[66]

I really couldn't have said it better myself and who better to believe than the Queen of Pop? Don't believe everything you see on social media where everyone is putting their best foot forward. We're all still human.

So go forth my friends and be the best humans that you can be. Remember to slow it down and take time to think. Enjoy the world in front of you and try your best not to get yelled at by Beyonce. And if you do get yelled at by Beyonce, then please tell me about it because that's a story I'd like to hear. Above all, treat each other with kindness. And don't forget to treat yourself with kindness as well.

JOSH GUNDERSON

about the author

Josh Gunderson is a graduate of Salem State University in Massachusetts where he earned his BA in both English and Theatre. He is an educational speaker specializing in Internet safety and bullying prevention. Since 2009 he has spoken to over one million students, parents and educators on these topics. He is the host of *The Millennial Agenda Podcast,* proprietor of *The Hot Mess Press Co* on Etsy, and the strange mind behind the blog *Avoiding Neverland.*

He has previously written <u>Cyberbullying: Perpetrators, Bystanders and Victims</u> and <u>You're Doing It Wrong: A Mixtape Memoir</u> which are both available wherever you buy books.

Josh currently resides in Orlando, FL where he can usually be found running around theme parks in his free time. Otherwise, he is sitting at home with his three cats with his nose buried in one of the millions of books on his to-read list and ignoring his currently in-progress novel.

More information about Josh's educational programs can be found on his website at www.joshgunderson.com. Free resources for educators and parents can be found on his (slightly more) professional blog *Breaking Down Digital Walls* at www.digitalwalls.org.

notes

1 "The Common Sense Census: Media Use By Teens and Tweens," Common Sense Media, 2019,
https://www.commonsensemedia.org/sites/default/files/uploads/research/2019-census-8-to-18-full-report-updated.pdf
2 "The Common Sense Census: Plugged-In Parents of Tweens and Tweens," Common Sense Media, 2016,
https://www.commonsensemedia.org/sites/default/files/uploads/research/common-sense-parent-census_whitepaper_new-for-web.pdf
3 "China Brings 5G to Mount Everest," Slate.com, July 29, 2020,
https://slate.com/technology/2020/07/mount-everest-5g-china-tibet-nepal-border.html
4 Children's Online Privacy Protection Act of 1998, 15 U.S.C. 6501–6505 https://www.ftc.gov/enforcement/rules/rulemaking-regulatory-reform-proceedings/childrens-online-privacy-protection-rule
5Gowen Walsh, Heather, "Getting Kids to Follow the Rules," Parent.com, October 6, 2013,
https://www.parents.com/kids/discipline/setting-limits/getting-kids-to-follow-the-rules/
6 Stephens, Richard, "Swearing is Actually A Sign of More Intelligence - Not Less- Say Scientists," Science Alert, February 2, 2017,
https://www.sciencealert.com/swearing-is-a-sign-of-more-intelligence-not-less-say-scientists
7 "Gen Z's Most Loved Brands," https://morningconsult.com/most-loved-brands-genz/
8 Katja Vujić, "A Guide to the Many, Many Scandals of James Charles," The Cut, May 12, 2021,
https://www.thecut.com/article/james-charles-allegations-and-accusations-explained.html
9 Siems, Eli, "Jailed for Facebook Post: 19-Year-Old Justin Carter, State Sensitivity and the Half-Million Dollar Bail," National Coalition Against Censorship, July 10, 2013,
https://ncac.org/news/blog/jailed-for-a-facebook-post-19-year-old-justin-carter-state-sensitivity-and-the-half-million-dollar-bail
10 Shontell, Alyson, "When a Teen's 'Sarcastic' Facebook Message Goes Terribly Wrong," Business Insider, July 8, 2013,

https://www.businessinsider.com/teen-justin-carter-faces-trial-and-jail-for-facebook-comment-2013-7

11 Sanders, Austin, "Felony Charges Dropped in 'Facebook Threat' Case," Austin Chronicle, April 6, 2018, https://www.austinchronicle.com/daily/news/2018-04-06/felony-charges-dropped-in-facebook-threat-case/

12 "Rise in Burglary Linked to Austerity and Social Media," Calder Security, https://www.caldersecurity.co.uk/rise-in-burglary-linked-to-austerity-and-social-media/

13 Almasy, Steve, "Houston Burglary Gang Used Social Media to Find Houses to Hit With High-End Art to Steal, Police Say," July 24, 2019, cnn.com/2019/07/24/us/houston-burglary-gang-social-media-stakeouts/index.html

14 "Yes, College Admissions Officers Are Looking At Social Media," IvyWise, January 13, 2020, https://www.ivywise.com/blog/yes-college-admissions-officers-are-looking-at-social-media/

15 Curtin, Melanie, "54 Percent of Employers Have Eliminated a Candidate Based on Social Media," Inc.com, January 9, 2020, https://www.inc.com/melanie-curtin/54-percent-of-employers-have-eliminated-a-candidate-based-on-social-media-time-to-clean-up-your-feed-and-tags.html

16 "The Bill of Rights: A Transcription," https://www.archives.gov/founding-docs/bill-of-rights-transcript

17 "What Type of Speech Is Not Protected by the First Amendment," https://www.hg.org/legal-articles/what-type-of-speech-is-not-protected-by-the-first-amendment-34258

18 Elhauge, Einer, "The First Amendment Doesn't Protect Donald's Incitement," The Washington Post, January 21, 2021, https://www.washingtonpost.com/outlook/2021/01/14/trump-brandenburg-impeachment-first-amendment/

19 Hannah, Maddie, "Does Twitter's Ban Violate Trump's Free Speech Rights," The Philadelphia Inquirer, January 9, 2021, https://www.inquirer.com/news/twitter-bans-trump-free-speech-first-amendment-20210109.html

20 "Watts v. United States" https://www.oyez.org/cases/1968/1107

21 18 U.S.C. § 871(a) provides: "Whoever knowingly and willfully deposits for conveyance in the mail or for a delivery from any post office or by any letter carrier any letter, paper, writing, print, missive, or document containing any threat to take the life of or to inflict bodily harm upon the President of the United States, the President-elect, the Vice President or other officer next in the order of succession to the office of President of the United States, or the Vice President-elect, or knowingly and willfully otherwise makes any such threat against the President, President-elect, Vice President or other officer next in the order of succession to the office of President, or Vice President-elect, shall be fined not more than $1,000 or imprisoned not more than five years, or both."

22 Hudson Jr, David, "Watts v. United States (1969), MTSU.edu, 2009, https://www.mtsu.edu/first-amendment/article/707/watts-v-united-states

23 Roley, Amanda "When Does Free Speech Become Harassment?" KREM.com, July 13, 2017, https://www.krem.com/article/news/verify/verify-when-does-free-speech-become-harassment/293-456501762

24 HumorCode.com, "What Are the Funniest Cities in the United States," http://humorcode.com/wp-content/uploads/2014/04/humor-code-funniest-cities-in-america.pdf

25 Henderson, Sarah, "Laughter and Learning: Humor Boosts Retention," Edutopia.com, March 31, 2015, https://www.edutopia.org/blog/laughter-learning-humor-boosts-retention-sarah-henderson

26 Siems, Eli, "Jailed for Facebook Post: 19-Year-Old Justin Carter, State Sensitivity and the Half-Million Dollar Bail," National Coalition Against Censorship, July 10, 2013, https://ncac.org/news/blog/jailed-for-a-facebook-post-19-year-old-justin-carter-state-sensitivity-and-the-half-million-dollar-bail

27 Abdelaziz, Salma, "Teen Arrested for Tweeting Airline Terror Threat, CNN, April 14, 2014, https://www.cnn.com/2014/04/14/travel/dutch-teen-arrest-american-airlines-terror-threat-tweet/index.html

28 Wordsworth, Araminta, "Dutch Teen's Prank Terrorist Tweet Blows Up In Airline's Face," National Post, April 17, 2014,

https://nationalpost.com/opinion/dutch-teens-prank-terrorist-tweet-blows-up-in-airlines-face

29 Nolan, Emma, "From Gina Carano to Roseanne Barr, These Celebs Were Fired By Disney Over Scandals", Newsweek, February 16, 2021, https://www.newsweek.com/celebs-fired-disney-scandals-gina-carano-roseanne-barr-pewdiepie-jake-paul-james-gunn-1569612

30 Pilkington, Ed, "Justine Sacco, PR Executive Fired Over Racist Tweet, 'Ashamed,'" The Guardian, December 22, 2013, https://www.theguardian.com/world/2013/dec/22/pr-exec-fired-racist-tweet-aids-africa-apology

31 McKeon, Kelsey, "5 Personal Branding Tips for Your Job Search," The Manifest, April 28, 2020, https://themanifest.com/digital-marketing/5-personal-branding-tips-job-search

32 Wagner, Meg, "Texas Teen Fired From Pizza Shop," New York Daily News, February 9, 2015, https://www.nydailynews.com/news/national/texas-teen-fired-f-k-a-pizza-shop-job-tweets-article-1.2108603

33 Staff Reporter, "Twitter Firing Jet's Pizza," Jobs & Hire, February 12, 2015, https://www.jobsnhire.com/articles/18852/20150212/twitter-firing-jets-pizza-texas-teenager-gets-fired-on-twitter-after-complaining-about-her-new-job.htm

34 Moye, David, "Starbucks Barista Fired For Tweeting Customer's 'Crazy' Order," Huffpost, May 14, 2021, https://www.huffpost.com/entry/starbucks-employee-fired-frappuccino_l_609e9ea7e4b014bd0cab9d60

35 "Yes, College Admissions Officers Are Looking At Social Media," IvyWise, January 13, 2020, https://www.ivywise.com/blog/yes-college-admissions-officers-are-looking-at-social-media/

36 Greenspan, Rachel, "Kombucha Girl Brittany Tomlinson on Life After a Viral Meme," TIME, December 19, 2019, https://time.com/5744175/kombucha-girl-tiktok-brittany-tomlinson-interview/

37 Pitt, Simon, "The Internet Is Only Permanent When You Don't Want it to Be," OneZero, May 29, 2020, https://onezero.medium.com/the-Internet-is-only-permanent-when-you-dont-want-it-to-be-6f5127c6e27f
38 Ockerman, Emma, "Here Are the Homophobic Tweets Kevin Hart's Not Sorry For," Vice News, December 7, 2018, https://www.vice.com/en/article/zmdwk3/here-are-the-homophobic-tweets-kevin-harts-not-sorry-for
39 Fleming Jr, Mark, "What 'Guardians' Director James Gun Learned From High-Profile Firing," Deadline, May 15, 2019, https://deadline.com/2018/07/james-gunn-fired-guardians-of-the-galaxy-disney-offensive-tweets-1202430392/
40 "Snapchat Settles FTC Charges That Promises of Disappearing Messages Were False," Federal Trade Commission Press Release, May 8, 2014, https://www.ftc.gov/news-events/press-releases/2014/05/snapchat-settles-ftc-charges-promises-disappearing-messages-were
41 Holpuch, Amanda, "Snapchat Admits to Handing Over Uno-pened 'Snaps' to US Law Enforcement, The Guardian, October 15, 2013, https://www.theguardian.com/world/2013/oct/15/snapchat-hands-snaps-pictures-to-federal-law-enforcement
42 Hoppe, Ian, "The Snappening: Over 200,000 Nude Snapchat Images Leaked," Birmingham Real-Time News, October 10, 2014, https://www.al.com/news/birmingham/2014/10/the_snappening_hundreds_of_tho.html
43 Gallagher, Billy, "How Reggie Brown Invented Snapchat, TechCrunch, February 10, 2018, https://techcrunch.com/2018/02/10/the-birth-of-snapchat/
44 Vogels, Josey, "Textual Gratification: Quill or Keypad, It's All About Sex," The Globe and Mail, May 3, 2004, https://www.theglobeandmail.com/technology/textual-gratification-quill-or-keypad-its-all-about-sex/article1136823/
45 Gollayan, Christian, "My Quest For Instagram Stardom Left Me In Financial Ruin," New York Post, March 3, 2018, https://nypost.com/2018/03/03/my-quest-for-instagram-stardom-left-me-in-financial-ruin/

46 Corradetti, Alex, "'Don't Keep It A Secret': Spike in Romance & Catfish Scams, Reports BBB," WKRN.com, May 22, 2021, https://www.wkrn.com/news/dont-keep-it-a-secret-spike-in-romance-catfish-scams-reports-bbb/

47 Blaschka, Amy, "This is Why You Need To Turn Off Your Social Media Notifications," Forbes, September 21, 2020, https://www.forbes.com/sites/amyblaschka/2020/09/21/this-is-why-you-need-to-turn-off-social-media-notifications

48 "US Adults Added 1 Hour of Digital Time in 2020" eMarketer, January 26, 2021, https://www.emarketer.com/content/us-adults-added-1-hour-of-digital-time-2020?ecid=NL1001

49 "The Common Sense Census: Media Use By Teens and Tweens," Common Sense Media, 2019, https://www.commonsensemedia.org/sites/default/files/uploads/research/2019-census-8-to-18-full-report-updated.pdf

50 Lewis, Hilary, "Beyonce Tells Fan: 'Put That Damn Camera Down!' Hollywood Reporter, July 17, 2013, https://www.hollywoodreporter.com/news/music-news/beyonce-tells-fan-put-damn-587642/

51 Zimdars, Melissa, "Fasle, Misleading, Clickbait-y, and/or Satirical 'News' Sources' Merrimack College, 2016, https://docs.google.com/document/d/10eA5-mCZLSS4MQY5QGb5ewC3VAL6pLkT53V_81ZyitM/preview

52 Alexander, Bryan, "Seth Walsh, Gay Boy Bullied into Suicide, Remembered," TIME Magazine, October 2, 2010, http://content.time.com/time/nation/article/0,8599,2023083,00.html

53 Gordon, Sherri, "Why Victims of Bullying Often Suffer in Silence," Verywell Family, February 27, 2021, https://www.verywellfamily.com/reasons-why-victims-of-bullying-do-not-tell-460784

54 "Selfie Tragedy Forever Impacts Those Left Behind," Union Pacific, December 8, 2016, https://www.up.com/aboutup/community/inside_track/selfie-tragedy-12-7-2016.htm

55 Hall, John, "Selfie-Obsessed Romanian Teen Bursts Into Flames When She Touched Live Wire," Daily Mail, May 12, 2015, https://www.dailymail.co.uk/news/article-3078178/Romanian-

selfie-obsessed-teen-burst-flames-touching-live-wire-climbing-train-ultimate-photo-herself.html

56 Associated Press, "Driver That Caused Fatal Traffic Pileup in Missouri Was Texting Before Crash," Syracuse.com, December 12, 2011,
https://www.syracuse.com/news/2011/12/driver_that_caused_fatal_traff.html

57 Associated Press, "NTSB: Driver Texted 11 Times Before Deadly Crash," CBS News, December 13, 2011,
https://www.cbsnews.com/news/ntsb-driver-texted-11-times-before-deadly-crash/

58 https://www.nsc.org/getmedia/88c97198-b7f3-4acd-a294-6391e3b8b56c/undercounted-is-underinvested.pdf

59 https://www.teendriversource.org/teen-crash-risks-prevention/distracted-driving/cell-phones

60 https://www.edgarsnyder.com/car-accident/cause-of-accident/cell-phone/cell-phone-statistics.html

61 Ameen, Luke, "The 25 Scariest Texting and Driving Statistics," IceBike, February 14th, 2017, https://www.icebike.org/texting-and-driving/

62 Hilliard, Jill "Social Media Addiction", Addiction Center, June 15, 2021, https://www.addictioncenter.com/drugs/social-media-addiction/

63 Hunt MG, Marx R, Lipson C, Young J. No more FOMO: Limiting social media decreases loneliness and depression. J Soc Clin Psychol. 2018;37(10):751-768. doi:10.1521/jscp.2018.37.10.751

64 Ibid, footnote 69

65 Dalton, Andrew, "Britney Spears Tells Judge: 'I Want My Life Back,'" APNews.com, June 23, 2021,
https://apnews.com/article/britney-spears-conservatorship-hearing-575ce4b7be0465603ad2e0e5df970809

66 https://www.instagram.com/p/CQhP9A7gIzE/

www.ingramcontent.com/pod-product-compliance
Lightning Source LLC
LaVergne TN
LVHW051340050326
832903LV00031B/3645